"The peaceful cover well expresses Levine and effective approach to resolving anxiety and phobias in children with developmental difficulties. By showing how to break down a child's fears into more tolerably sized 'chunks,' they provide a means of keeping the child engaged in the therapeutic work, preventing the frequent dropouts of behavioral treatment. While they designed a method for children with special needs, it will enhance the treatment of any child or teen with anxiety or phobias. Clear and direct enough to instruct a beginning clinician, it is rich and innovative enough to teach experienced therapists."

—Richard Bromfield, PhD, Harvard Medical School, author
of Doing Therapy with Children and Adolescents with
Asperger Syndrome and Embracing Asperger's

"Too often children with autism are viewed through the lens of the condition, with their challenges seen purely as 'behavior.' However, anxiety is such a key issue for so many individuals on the autism spectrum that it becomes essential to treat it as an individual and individualized 'thing' rather than largely disregarded simply as part of the diagnosis. This book is a welcome and much-needed addition to a field of literature on treating the core symptoms of autism in an emotionally centred and child-friendly way. Levine and Chedd have made a largely misunderstood but essential part of autism treatment accessible to professionals and parents alike. They offer a practical, effective way to approach and treat anxiety in autism. Most importantly, children and the professionals that treat them will also have great fun attacking anxiety together!"

—Ruth Glynne-Owen, Founder and Chief Executive,
Speur-Ghlan Early Intervention Service, Scotland

"This is a lovely book, which has many ideas applicable to neurotypical children as well. Brilliant for toddlers tantrumming (I have toddler grandsons aged one and two, and am already having conversations with the hand-dryer in the church lavatory—wonderful!)."

—Carolyn Holleyman, Grandmother of three toddler boys

ATTACKING ANXIETY

A Step-by-Step Guide to an Engaging
Approach to Treating Anxiety and
Phobias in Children with Autism and
Other Developmental Disabilities

KAREN LEVINE AND NAOMI CHEDD

Jessica Kingsley *Publishers*
London and Philadelphia

First published in 2015
by Jessica Kingsley Publishers
73 Collier Street
London N1 9BE, UK
and
400 Market Street, Suite 400
Philadelphia, PA 19106, USA

www.jkp.com

Copyright © Karen Levine and Naomi Chedd 2015

Front cover image source: Shutterstock®.

Library of Congress Cataloging in Publication Data
Levine, Karen, 1959-
  Attacking anxiety : a step-by-step guide to an Engaging
approach to treating anxiety and phobias in
children with autism and other developmental disabilities / Karen Levine and Naomi Chedd.
    pages cm
  Includes bibliographical references and index.
  ISBN 978-1-84905-788-2 (alk. paper)
  1. Anxiety in children--Treatment. 2. Autistic children--
Treatment. 3. Cognitive therapy for children. I.
Chedd, Naomi, 1952- II. Title.
  RJ506.A58L48 2015
  618.92'8522--dc23
                              2015002073

British Library Cataloguing in Publication Data
A CIP catalogue record for this book is available from the British Library

ISBN 978 1 84905 788 2
eISBN 978 1 78450 044 3

Printed and bound in Great Britain

MIX
Paper from
responsible sources
FSC
www.fsc.org   FSC® C013056

For the children and families impacted by phobias.
KL

For the students and staff of the Massachusetts
Hospital School, Canton, MA.
NC

ACKNOWLEDGEMENTS

We want to thank Diane Twachtman-Cullen, Ph.D., CCC-SLP, Editor-in-Chief of *Autism Spectrum Quarterly* for publishing an earlier version of this book in a three-article series and for her encouragement in developing the articles into a book.

We also want to thank Elizabeth Stringer-Keefe, Assistant Professor of Special Education, Graduate School of Education, Lesley University, for her help in the school collaboration section in Chapter 11.

We want to thank our editor, Rachel Menzies, for her enthusiasm about this book as well as her patience.

We are grateful to the vast number of clinicians and researchers from the fields of developmental psychology, behavioral psychology, play therapy, CBT and DIR/Floortime® (The Developmental, Individual Difference Relationship-based model), who have created large bodies of literature on which our work is founded.

We are especially grateful to the families who have faith in us as we play and collaborate with them and their children in sometimes seemingly unusual ways—tossing around wads of tissue and toy bugs, pretending to be mortified by plastic cheese, glue and glitter, and playfully joining them in their aversions to clowns, cats and crayons. We are most grateful to the children themselves, who bravely attack and often conquer their fears, and from whom we continue to learn every day. We are extraordinarily lucky to have them in our lives.

KL and NC

CONTENTS

PREFACE

Consider this scenario: It is time for recess at daycare and I (KL) am juggling and struggling with 12 toddlers, helping them squeeze into their snowsuits, boots, hats, and mittens. I, along with these miniature astronauts, am going through our daily routine, preparing for Planet Playground on a blustery New England winter afternoon. By the time I have just about finished bundling up the last few, the first ones dressed are throwing themselves on the floor, kicking off their boots, complaining and crying, clearly uncomfortable and becoming more and more distressed. So of course it takes much longer to get them ready. Their restlessness and agitation are building and their cooperation is vanishing. This scene repeats itself on a daily basis, sometimes two or even three times on some days, leaving everyone exhausted and depleted.

One day, in the midst of just such a moment, without any forethought—maybe to ease my own frustration and distress—I lay down on the floor and had a full-blown pretend tantrum, playfully mimicking the ones my small charges treated me to regularly. "NO! NO!" I protested, as I kicked off my Birkenstocks. "STOP! NO HAT!" I exclaimed, as I threw my hat under the table. Much to my surprise, several toddlers stopped in their tracks and gathered around me. They quickly fetched my shoes, hat and gloves from the farthest reaches of the room, saying in a knowing, adult-like corrective tone, "Shoes ON, Karen… Hat ON!" I felt like

Gulliver in Lilliput, as these tiny beings worked together, calmly and collaboratively, to put me back together. "Wait a second," I thought, as I played along with this role reversal, "Weren't *you* the very same munchkins who were grousing about getting dressed only moments ago?"

When I resumed the original task, it was much easier. Although I didn't fully understand what had happened or why there had been such a shift, I knew I was on to something. I continued to experiment in the following weeks and months, playing out their typical toddler "traumas" and natural fearful responses, like saying goodbye to their parents in the morning, their fears of spiders and bugs, anticipation of doctor visits, and worries about strange noises or the dark at naptime.

Years later, in my work with children with developmental challenges, including autism, I continued to refine and use these same kinds of approaches, incorporating many cognitive behavioral approaches, such as gradual exposure and progressive desensitization, as well as the social/emotional components in the DIR/Floortime® (The Developmental, Individual Difference Relationship-based model) approach. I continued to see a positive impact and forged trusting, mutually enjoyable relationships with the children I treated.

We have focused our work (and this book) on treating fears and phobias because it can be helpful to children and families. At the same time, it is something we deeply enjoy doing. Last week I was consulting in a classroom for children with special needs, and they were having a "balloon party." One boy was terrified of balloons, and immediately ran the other way while wincing and covering his ears. I intercepted him, frowned and directed my displeasure to the balloons too, whisper-yelling, "NO balloons! TOO LOUD! Hurts my ears!" while shaking my finger at the offending balloons, then covering my ears too. My fearful little friend stopped crying, watched me closely, and when I did it again, he smiled. We did this together several times and eventually he was laughing, watching and then joining me in scolding the balloons. He inched a little closer, shook his finger and boldly told the balloons they were "TOO LOUD." In a short time he joined his classmates and carried on. It was a victory for him, fun for his peers, and a relief for his teacher. But it was also fun and satisfying for me—a member of his "winning team," conquering his fear together.

Now consider this scenario:

Although I (NC) didn't think so at the time, I was a lucky kid. As the daughter of two librarians who valued travel above all else, I was fortunate to see a lot of the country, albeit from the back seat of 10-year-old Chevy, with my annoying older brother Jay badgering me every inch of the way. My father did the driving while my mother, the navigator, hoarded quarters for tolls and wrestled with those unwieldy maps, while telling my dad which highways to take and where to get off, both literally and figuratively. Moving fast and efficiently from one place to another was a major challenge. Remember: this was decades before Mapquest, EZ Pass and the ubiquitous GPS.

On occasion… no; on many occasions, my parents would have… let's say "differences of opinion" about the best route, where to stop for gas, when to stop for the night, where to eat, what time to set off the morning, and every other subject about which there could be a debate. Although Jay and I pestered each other and argued constantly, we did agree on one thing: we couldn't stand listening to our parents' bickering, especially about things that seemed unimportant, even ridiculous, like which diner looked the cleanest or whether we could make it another 50 miles before it got dark. We never could of course, and each parent would blame the other.

Sometimes, after we pulled into a motel—after a major discussion, naturally, causing us to miss the ones with pools—and parked the car, Jay would climb into the driver's seat and I would hop in right beside him. Now *we* were the parents! "Florence, are you absolutely *sure* this is the right exit? I think it's the next one," Jay would shout in his best Dad voice. "Don't worry Allan; I know what I'm doing," I'd snap back, very Mom-like. "I hope you have enough quarters," he would warn me, and I would respond acerbically, "I actually don't... and who told you to get in the exact change lane anyway?" And on and on we went, joyfully playing out the events, conversations, and conflicts of our travels that day and laughing all the way.

We did this at home as well, right in our driveway, or at the dining room table, or at bedtime, revisiting and re-enacting all kinds of family dramas, especially the ones we found disturbing or puzzling and some that were just plain ridiculous. We thought we were hilarious.

But this exercise was more than a couple of silly little kids playing at being grown-ups. I know this now. We were learning to understand our feelings and becoming more able to manage and not become overwhelmed by the distress we felt when we observed situations that were confusing or troubling for us. By repeatedly dramatizing, exaggerating and embellishing certain anxiety-causing events in a comical fashion, together, and in a way that only we could understand, with hilarity that we shared, we became more able to tolerate and even appreciate our parents' struggles and our parents, themselves. The sting had evaporated.

Our parents, perhaps unaware of how we perceived them and how strong their influence was, often observed our antics and even joined in on occasion. They laughed and learned something too, in a way that was palatable, non-threatening and endlessly entertaining for the entire family.

As children my brother and I had naturally and spontaneously happened upon role playing of these anxiety-provoking scenarios, using shared humor to decrease our distress around them. They are the tools that form the basis of the model in this book.

Fast forward several decades.

We continued to elaborate on this model together, tailoring it for children with various developmental challenges, writing about it in *Replays: Using Play to Enhance Emotional and Behavioral Development for Children with Autism Spectrum Disorders* (Levine and Chedd 2006). We have become increasingly aware of the very substantial impact of children's fears and phobias on family well-being, child behavior and participation in school and home activities. We found that couching the approaches we had developed in *Replays* within a targeted, multi-faceted gradual exposure framework was guiding our work—our direct work with children as well as with their family and school teams. It is our hope that in writing this book we are helping alleviate children's distress around predictable fears in ways that are understandable and accessible to families and clinicians.

References

Levine, K. and Chedd, N. (2006) *Replays: Using Play to Enhance Emotional and Behavioral Development for Children with Autism Spectrum Disorders.* London: Jessica Kingsley Publishers.

CHAPTER 1

WHAT IS A PHOBIA AND HOW DO PHOBIAS EVOLVE OVER TIME?

The oldest and strongest emotion of mankind is fear.
H.P. LOVECRAFT

This chapter provides background, explaining first what a phobia is, how phobias can manifest in children with autism spectrum disorder (ASD), and how phobias evolve over time. The concept of phobias spreading to triggers associated with the initial trigger will be discussed, with several examples, since understanding this common occurrence is key to understanding the treatment. Anticipatory anxiety, or "fear of fear" is another key consideration in treatment and will be explained. This chapter provides the background and rationale needed to access and engage in the treatment process, which comprises the rest of the book.

What is a phobia?

Consider the following:

— A four-year-old who loves his father screams and runs away when he coughs or laughs.

— A toddler shrieks in distress every time she has her hair washed and even when her parents begin to get her ready for a bath.

— A first-grader is scared of the lunch bell and spends the entire morning at school worrying and anticipating it.

— An eight-year-old panics when approaching the doctor's office and needs to be sedated, even for routine medical care.

— A third-grader dreads going to school on special-event days and has trouble sleeping in the days or even weeks leading up to them.

— A student is so afraid of making a mistake that he refuses to do any math homework, classwork or take tests.

— A young athlete is so worried about losing that she avoids playing any team sports or competitive games with peers.

These reactions all seem out of proportion in relation to any real threat or danger. However, these children experience them as real and extremely disturbing, and rational explanations and reassurance rarely help diminish those responses. Moreover, they can have a dramatic and negative impact on the child's quality of life and those who care for them, teach them, and want to be their friends.

Adaptive and maladaptive fears

Experiencing fear is normal. It is a fact of life for every one of us. Fear—healthy fear—is also adaptive. Evolutionarily, survival of the human race depends on it. If we did not fear and avoid truly dangerous situations or proceed with extreme caution and preparedness in the face of a potential threat, we would not live very long. The great majority of us develop a healthy sense of fear. We do not jump off the top of a ten-story building, plunge our hands into a fire, or drive at 100 miles per hour. We are scared for our lives and we should be. These situations are dangerous and life-threatening. If we learn that a major hurricane or snowstorm is about to hit our part of the world, we do everything we can to protect ourselves, our families, and our property. We prepare for the worst. We may even abandon our homes and belongings if the perceived threat is too great, because the desire for self-preservation and the drive to survive are so strong. From an evolutionary perspective, animals and early humans that did not experience fear did not survive. (Now, of course, children without sufficient safety awareness, like many with autism, are provided with protection from others.)

Phobias are extreme and persistent fear responses to objects and events that don't pose a real danger—or certainly not as much as imagined. Interestingly, many children with ASD also have diminished fear responses to some situations that are truly dangerous. The child terrified of getting into the bathtub may lack safety awareness about busy streets or heights. The child who tries to bolt into the street, oblivious to cars, may also run the other way upon hearing the sound of the electric toothbrush or have an intense fear of cheese, small wind-up toys, or butterflies. Extreme fears or phobias in children with ASD, as in the general population, often defy logic, which can be extremely puzzling and frustrating for those who care for them or spend time with them. An eight-year-old who loves sharks, lizards, and snakes quivers and recoils when he sees a picture of a particular character in a popular children's book series. A ten-year-old with Asperger's, afraid of germs and swear words, takes tremendous risks when climbing trees and jumping from high places, He recently asked, "Why is it my fears are all about the silly irrational things?" As with many adults and children with phobias, he is quite bright and recognizes that his reactions defy reason. But this does not diminish their power over him and his extreme reactions.

How fear and coping skills develop in children with and without ASD or other developmental disabilities

Beginning in infancy we learn what is and isn't dangerous or threatening through our interactions with our environment and especially our relationships with others. Infants are scared of all sorts of things that are not dangerous—a loud sound, a falling leaf, a bug, a new face, a momentary separation from a parent. Caregivers comfort them through a range of physical means, holding, rocking, singing, and using a range of social means, such as gazing and smiling at them and talking to them calmly. Infants who orient to and can read these nonverbal social cues look to caregivers increasingly for soothing when they are scared. Even within their first few months of life, typically developing infants look to caregivers' faces and attune to their voices when confronted with neutral or potentially threatening stimuli, such as a new person entering the room or an unfamiliar sound, to determine if there is danger. When they are already scared or distressed, such as when they fall down or an unfamiliar person picks them up, infants are comforted by both self-soothing actions (e.g. thumb sucking) and through interpreting the caregiver's verbal and nonverbal cues, giving their own cues back, re-interpreting the new cues caregivers send. Co-regulation is the term for this dynamic process (Fogel 1993), which has also been called a dynamic ever subtly shifting "dance" between parent and infant (Tronick and Beeghly 2011).

Consider an infant who becomes frightened at the sound of his grandfather's loud cough, and with a wrinkled brow, reddening face, and about to cry, turns to his father who is holding him. Gazing back at his baby, the father says in a calm, reassuring voice, "Grandpa's just coughing, my dear. There, there," and the baby then returns the father's gaze and calms a bit...until he hears another jarring cough and again begins to cry. His father comforts him again, repeating, "There, there. Everything is fine," with the same reassuring look while swaying him gently. The baby calms and looks up to his father again and then lays his head down, relaxing and releasing his tension. The next time his grandfather coughs, the baby startles slightly, but does not become distressed. He has learned from his father's vocal and nonverbal cues and their repeated co-regulation that that the coughing sound is not a threat.

Now in contrast, consider another similarly distressed infant who cannot read the father's cues or can't sufficiently interpret them so they have a soothing effect. Maybe this baby also has more difficulty calming and naturally reacts more dramatically when he hears loud noises, like coughing. Any or all of these factors will cause this baby to become extremely disturbed each time his grandfather coughs. His repeated, intense distress creates a pattern—a learned fear response to coughing that is not easily "unlearned."

As infants develop, they continue to interpret what is dangerous, as well as learning how to soothe through reading nonverbal cues and eventually, through understanding verbal language. They ask and receive reassurance repeatedly from their parents and other caregivers. A toddler seeing snow for the first time might say "Mamma!" with alarm, alternating looking at the snow to looking at her mother, pointing, and showing distress. Her mother reassures her, smiling, "It's just snow, honey." The toddler, having no idea what "snow" means or if it is dangerous, discerns that her mother is not scared from her facial expression, and reassuring tone, which she has learned to interpret over time, and concludes that snow is not dangerous.

Responses change over time

Toddlers learn and revise their own initial responses based on reading the cues of all those around them. They observe that, "Mommy is smiling and talking to the nurse, not crying like me after my shot, so maybe I'm fine," or "My brother smiled and jumped up and down when he saw that rabbit hop across the lawn. I guess rabbits are safe." Toddlers and preschoolers instantly look for adult reactions after they take a tumble to determine if it is a crisis or just a minor setback. It is as if they are thinking, "I might be badly hurt! Let me figure this out. What are the adults doing? Daddy is calm. He just smiled at me and went back to chatting with his friend. So I must be OK!" Or conversely, "Mommy looks like she's about to cry. I must be hurt! I'm going to cry."

A toddler with limited social skills, however, might shriek with alarm at the sight of snow, as the typically developing toddler above, yet without the intuitive capacity to "ask" his mother if it is dangerous, or interpret her cues. If he goes outside and enjoys the snow, his fear will likely diminish; however, if he doesn't like the sensation, he might develop a consistent pattern of fear whenever he sees snow. He might, unlike his typically developing counterpart, become very fearful after having a shot, as he may not be able to read the reassuring cues of the adults around him. Conversely, not being able to read social cues that signal actual danger likely contributes to lack of fear that is adaptive, such as fear of running into the street, or fear of climbing up too high on the rocks.

Between two and three years of age, children increasingly engage in spontaneous pretend play. They naturally pretend and replay their day-to-day experiences, especially those that are emotionally meaningful to them. One of us (KL) was a daycare provider for many years and a favorite game amongst the toddlers was to get on a riding toy, or sling on a scarf or bag and say, "Bye-bye—Go work," and repeatedly walk away, then come back. This was part of their daily experience. Toddlers and preschoolers love to play doctor, often exaggerating the emotionally salient parts ("You need 1000 shots!" "You have to stay in bed for two years!"). When an event impacts an entire community, such as a huge storm, a power outage, or some kind of trauma, one sees children playing through these events over and over, individually and together.

We were consulting in elementary schools after the 9/11 attacks and observed children drawing people falling off skyscrapers, building towers with blocks and flying toy planes into them. Teachers would ask us if this was "OK," and "normal," as adults worry and wonder if this kind of play should be discouraged because it may instill more fear. In fact, helping children play out their experiences is often used therapeutically after a traumatic event, with a growing body of research supporting its positive impact (Dugan, Snow and Crowe 2010).

The French movie *Forbidden Games* (Clément 1952), about a five-year-old girl orphaned by a Nazi attack she witnesses, then taken in by a nearby family, features scenes of her playing out this trauma and creating, together with the ten-year-old boy of the family, a toy cemetery, their "forbidden game" as they try to process these hugely anxiety-provoking events. While sometimes some children can become "stuck on" playing out one event and not getting past it, for most children this kind of play, even repetitively, seems to help them cope with the overwhelming fearful emotions. (Note: pretend play around most day-to-day events is healthy and productive for children. However, some children do not want to play out some kinds of especially traumatic events, particularly while intense feelings of distress are present, and there are times when encouraging this is not recommended. Consulting a mental health specialist for children who have experienced trauma is warranted.)

Pretend play deficits

Toddlers and young children with ASD do not generally engage in this kind of spontaneous, emotionally engaging pretend play that incorporates their experiences (Hobson *et al.* 2013; 2014), even though many engage in some symbolic play that may replicate a scene they have seen on a video or have been taught.

As children develop they become increasingly able to converse, as parents, teachers, siblings, classmates, babysitters, help them: (1)

learn what is dangerous and what is not; (2) how to remain calm in the face of what feels a little frightening, such as a thunderstorm, a visit to the dentist, the dark, or passing a speeding fire truck with its siren blaring. And even as their language, pretend and role playing become more sophisticated, children continue to check in with caregivers through nonverbal means to co-regulate. But those with limited capacity for social use of language and play, including children with ASD, are less able to use these means to co-regulate.

To summarize, while infants become distressed easily in response to both major and minor stimuli, the developmental systems of nonverbal social cue reading, symbolic play, and social use of language are systems typically developing children use, both to help them soothe when they are afraid and to help them sort out which, of the things that cause them initial fear, are truly dangerous (an oncoming truck; running around in a parking lot) and what are not (a housefly; grandfather's cough). However, children with less developed social interactive, symbolic, and communication systems have less access to these means, which likely contributes to the greater number of children with anxiety and phobias among children with ASD.

How common are phobias?

Anxiety and phobias are fairly common in the general population. Some phobias are so common they are considered normative at a certain age, such as fear of the dark and of dogs among very young children. More severe anxiety and fears causing significant negative impact, are estimated to occur in about 5 percent to 10 percent of children (Kessler *et al.* 2005).

Anxiety and phobias are even more common in children with developmental disabilities, including ASD. About 40–44 percent of children on the autism spectrum were identified with specific phobias, and most had multiple phobias (van Steensel, Bogels and Perrin 2011; Leyfer *et al.* 2006). About 60–90 percent of children with Williams syndrome have specific phobias (Woodruff-Borden *et al.* 2010) and about 56–79 percent of children with Fragile-X syndrome, a genetic disorder that causes a range of learning, communication, and other developmental problems, also have an anxiety diagnosis (Garber, Visootsak and Warren 2008).

Why are phobias more common in children with ASD and some other developmental disabilities?

Previously we talked about developmental reasons that likely contribute to increased incidence of phobias among children with development difficulties, such as those that impact their capacity to interpret caregiver and peer social cues. Children with ASD or other developmental disabilities impacting social or communication domains, are not as easily able to access naturally occurring "co-regulation" tools of interaction that form the feedback loop that helps typically developing children sort out dangerous from non-dangerous experiences.

In addition, some developmental disabilities are thought to be associated with greater neurological reactivity. For example, many children with Williams' syndrome have a greater startle response to auditory stimuli, and their physiological systems become dysregulated more rapidly and are also harder to re-regulate. There is an association between ASD in one family member and anxiety disorders in other family members. For example, families in which there is an individual with bipolar disorder have an increased likelihood of having a family member with ASD (Sullivan, Magnusson and Reichenberg 2012). Hence there seems to be a genetic predisposition to greater emotional dysregulation in some individuals with ASD that is associated with mood and anxiety disorders. So some children with ASD or another developmental disability may be neurologically "wired" for anxiety and phobias, while having fewer ways to regulate and learn adaptive responses.

Are phobias in the ASD population harder to treat?

The probable causes for the higher incidence of these conditions does not mean phobias are any less treatable. In fact, we can design more effective treatment approaches for those with communication and social challenges by drawing upon the developmental routes to sorting out safe vs. unsafe in typical children. Helping children learn to co-regulate with adults, read and benefit from our social cues, and adapting how we communicate about their fear experiences by teaching/modeling how to use pretend and other forms of acting out their fear experiences, are key components of the treatment model we discuss throughout this book.

How does a phobia develop?

Often a child experiences an unexpected or unfamiliar object or event that he/she finds frightening, startling, or unpleasant. This object or event can then come to serve as a trigger for fear. For example, a child may have been startled upon hearing a balloon pop, or became uncomfortable and highly distressed during a hairwash when soap got in her eyes. Or a toddler happily approaches a dog and tries to pet him, but the dog barks loudly and jumps on the child.

The fear then spreads from the trigger event itself to a range of experiences associated with the event and especially leading up to the event. For example, the child who is initially afraid of thunderstorms becomes fearful of clouds in the sky because they sometimes lead to a thunderstorm. The child who is scared of having her hair washed becomes anxious when she hears the tub filling up. The toddler becomes fearful when he sees dogs in the distance or even on TV. All kinds of sensory experiences, including sounds, smells, and sights related to the trigger event, can become new sources of fear.

For many children fear begins to build as the time of the trigger event draws near. They become afraid that they will feel afraid. This is commonly known as anticipatory anxiety or "fear of fear."

The problem with avoidance

In the face of such a cycle, children naturally try to avoid the feared situation and anything associated with it. As a result, they don't learn coping strategies or get practice in tolerating the situation and getting through it safely. They don't find out that "There's nothing to worry about. Nothing bad will happen." It is normal for parents and other caregivers to protect the child and often they, too, go to extremes to avoid the feared situation. Sometimes this is a reasonable solution, as long as it doesn't limit the child or family's enjoyment of life. After all, a child who fears rollercoasters can easily and happily go through life without riding on one. A child who fears extreme heights can probably get away with not going mountain climbing, hang gliding or walking the 897 steps to the top of the Washington Monument! But complete avoidance isn't always possible, nor is it the best solution. For example, a child who fears fire drills can't stay home from school indefinitely, worrying that one day there might be one. A child may choose not to play a highly competitive sport, fearing that he will be on the losing team. But it would be nearly impossible and certainly not desirable to avoid all games or all competitions with peers.

Obsessive compulsive disorder (OCD)

Until recently OCD was considered to be a type of anxiety disorder, and it is still considered to be associated with anxiety. However, in the DSM-5 (American Psychiatric Association 2013), the latest rendition of the Diagnostic and Statistical Manual, OCD is described separately, in its own chapter, instead of included as a subset of Anxiety.

Obsessive thoughts are "stuck" in one's mind. Some obsessive thoughts are tied specifically to phobias as part of the child's anticipatory anxiety. For instance, children afraid of thunderstorms may ask in the morning, every single morning, and many, many times during the day what the weather is going to be, even if the sun is shining brightly. Children afraid of shots may ask every day if they will be having a shot, although for most typically developing, relatively healthy children, injections are only an occasional event.

The obsessive thoughts children have specifically related to their phobias are likely to diminish once the phobia has been treated successfully. Other obsessive thoughts are not directly related to a specific phobia that is outside of the thought, but might involve a fear of something the child might have done wrong (e.g. obsessive worry that they might have said a swear word). When devising treatment we find it helpful to think of obsessive thoughts as a fear of the event that might happen and treat the fear with gradual exposure in the same way. For the child obsessively worrying they might have said a swear word, pick some swear words acceptable to the child and family to practice writing, then whispering, then saying. Of course if the fear is of something unsafe happening one can't "practice" this, but one can similarly practice having a thought on purpose about it, or allowing the thought to enter one's mind and leave, in much the way one practices exposure to a phobia.

Compulsive actions, those that individuals feel "driven" to do, can seem unrelated to fears; however, the fear often escalates if the action cannot take place. For example, we had one patient who, once he coughed, felt the urge to cough an even number of times, and if he coughed an odd number, would force out another cough. He felt "something bad" might happen if he coughed an odd number of times. Another patient had to keep sharpening his pencils to keep them all at an even length. Each time he used one he couldn't resist the urge to check if it matched the others exactly, and if he found it was shorter, he felt an urge to sharpen all the other pencils. And another had to touch each desk every time she went up to the blackboard at the front of the class and again on the way back to her seat. If she missed one desk, she "had" to start all over.

There are even different types of OCD. For example, a child who scratched an itch on one side of her body felt she needed to scratch on the other side so she would feel "just right." Another child had to wash his hands multiple times during the day and bathed every morning and evening. A compulsion can also focus on how events transpire, such as feeling if one doesn't go in to school through a certain door, every single day, something bad will happen. The distress caused by even slight changes in schedule or locale is sometimes rooted in seemingly arbitrary changes to the order of events or environments that the child has gotten accustomed to and feels are compulsory.

Obsessive and compulsive traits are often present in children with ASD. In fact, "repetitive behaviors" are included in the DSM-5 diagnostic criteria for autism (American Psychiatric Association 2013). However, when repetitive behaviors are nonfunctional (flapping, rocking) disruptive to the child or others (hitting, yelling loudly) and when not engaging in them causes intense distress, considering them as one would a compulsion, or like a phobia about not doing them, can often lead directly to more effective treatment.

How are phobias and compulsions similar?

Consider the boy who felt he had to cough an even number of times. He was extremely fearful (phobic) about coughing an odd number of times. We were able to effectively treat this through gradual exposure combined with strategies to reduce his distress. We began with having him tell a Spiderman figure to "Cough only once," and Spiderman, with our voice-over help, was afraid and coughed twice. We made this playful and funny, giving the child control, instructing his mother how to play with Spiderman and what to do: "COUGH THREE TIMES! NOW!" and his mother would make Spiderman try very hard but "need" to add a fourth cough. Finally his mother said "SHOW me how to cough three times," and the child was able to show Spiderman. She then asked him to demonstrate coughing other odd numbers of times—one time, then five times, then seven. This child eventually noticed that he, like Spiderman, was actually OK coughing an odd number of times. This child commented on this with amazement "Hey, I coughed three times too!" and then proceeded to practice, feeling as proud and pleased as if he had just learned a cool new trick!

The brain, anxiety, and phobias

Neuroscientists are increasingly able to explain what happens in the brain when people experience fear, both as a response to a single event, and chronically over time. They are also beginning to understand certain brain differences in people with more vs. less fear. This branch of science, relating physiological and emotional experience to brain processes, is a rapidly developing field. New findings indicating that multiple brain areas and the dynamic connections between them, rather than static areas, impact and correlate with experience. Initial fears in early infancy relate to sensory experiences, and increasingly, to emotional ones— separation from primary caregiver, for example. The feedback loops and brain development resulting from such experiences become impacted as described by social and communication inputs from those surrounding the infant.

In spite of the complexity and so much still unknown, there is currently agreement that the amygdala, an early developing part of the brain in the temporal lobe, is involved in the experience of fear and development of anxiety. The amygdala processes sensory and emotional information and also sets off the "fight–flight" system. This brain center does not operate in isolation and connects from and to more advanced centers, including the cortex, which may respond logically. The amygdala processes sensory information immediately, creating an instant fight–flight response. But it also processes experience that takes a little longer, from the cortex to the amygdala, with additional information about the initial input.

Consider this: You are walking down the street and you hear a car backfire, giving off a sudden, loud popping sound. Immediately you think it's a gunshot or maybe an explosion. You startle, maybe even scream without meaning to (the initial sensory processing and reaction) and then you see the car, driving away, emitting a little smoke, and you realize what the sound was, that it is not dangerous, and your initial fear subsides.

The amygdala develops associations with certain sensory stimuli and "danger" responses from repeated experiences of the trigger and resulting distress. Gradual exposure to the same trigger without experiencing distress changes the response in the amygdala. So, if you worked at a job where you regularly heard cars backfiring, perhaps at a busy car repair shop, even though you might continue to startle, your startle response and the accompanying sensations would likely diminish in intensity and duration. However, if you were in a war zone where a sound does indeed indicate danger, your intense fight–flight response to loud sounds would be more likely to continue, even upon returning to a safe area, which is not uncommon in soldiers returning from war and others who have experienced or witnessed extreme trauma.

Consider a child hearing thunder for the first time and feeling intense fear. Then, upon seeing adults reacting calmly during many subsequent storms, understanding more about why they occur, watching videos of thunder and lightning, and chatting with others about it, the child is likely to respond to thunder without fear, presumably without activating the fight–flight response. However, if a child is unable to co-regulate due to neurological wiring, and to difficulties with understanding the language and nonverbal cues of family and friends, he/she will continue to respond to thunder fearfully.

The cornerstone of most phobia treatments, including the model described in this book, is based on this phenomenon, namely, that experiencing the feared trigger in the absence of anything bad happening, ultimately "retrains the brain." In the next chapter we will discuss treatment models that incorporate ways of helping children experience this in small manageable increments while remaining happy and calm.

A note on generalized anxiety

While this book is about treating specific fears and phobias, most children with specific fears also experience higher levels of general anxiety, or a higher "baseline" of anxiety much of the time. This may show up as increased preoccupation with and worry about a variety of things, and/or it may show up as form of difficulty settling down and focusing on work or play, persistent sleep problems, irritability, reactivity, restlessness or agitation. The more a child is able to communicate how he/she is feeling or thinking, the more clear it becomes that anxiety is the underlying cause of those external, observable behavioral difficulties. Working to reduce a child's baseline anxiety is important in and of itself, but it can also contribute to reducing the intensity of specific phobias.

When a child is experiencing a higher level of anxiety such as generally, at the beginning of the school year, or when a favorite teacher leaves or a new one arrives, or when there is a major change at home, old phobias may resurface or new ones may emerge. Often these are temporary and diminish as the child gets accustomed to the new situation or routine. But sometimes new patterns "stick," even when the circumstances triggering the increased fear reaction are no longer bothering the child. We saw one child who at the beginning of Kindergarten showed a huge increase in overall anxiety and also developed several specific phobias, including fear of the loudspeaker announcements, and of food smells. By November once he had become used to his new school and close to his teacher, the phobias gradually disappeared. The few that lingered, fear of Play-Doh and crayons, were relatively quick to treat using the model in this book.

New bedroom, new sleep problems

For example, a child who moved to a new bedroom because of the arrival of a baby began to have sleep problems, which is not surprising. But more than a year later, her sleep problems continued, although the child said, in fact, that her new room was bigger and she liked it much better than the old one. The child who used to be afraid of thunderstorms and then overcame the fear with the help of a CBT therapist once again begins to experience the same scary feelings after his best friend moves away.

One can think of this like the shock absorbers in a car: if the shock absorbers are worn and not working well, even small bumps in the road cause distress to the passengers, but when the shock absorbers are working well, the same small bumps are not problematic, and it takes a much bigger bump to be distressing. For a child whose emotional shock absorbers are not working well, that is, if their overall level of anxiety is high, it does not take as much to derail them. Bringing down their baseline level of anxiety, or getting their shock absorber system working better can reduce the little bumps, or fear trigger responses, to a much more manageable level.

There are several factors to consider when trying to reduce a child's overall level of baseline anxiety. These include the following:

1. Sleep

Insufficient sleep or major changes in sleep patterns tend to increase anxiety, and increased anxiety tends to make sleep more difficult, creating a vicious cycle. Many children have both anxiety and poor sleep habits, and it's difficult to tell if there is truly a cause and effect relationship. And of course, when children sleep poorly, so do their parents, and parents who are sleep-deprived are more likely to be more irritable and reactive, further adding fuel to the negative cycle. So addressing sleep problems, working closely with your child's pediatrician and/or other medical specialists, can help reduce baseline anxiety. There are excellent books about "sleep hygiene," including *Solve Your Child's Sleep Problems: New, Revised, and Expanded Edition* (Ferber 2006) and *Solving Sleep Problems in Children with Autism Spectrum Disorders: A Guide for Frazzled Families* (Katz and Malow 2014). Your child's pediatrician may have additional recommendations.

2. Exercise

An increasing number of studies point to the value of regular exercise in reducing anxiety in the general population (e.g. Herring, O'Connor and Dishman 2010), and in children, although the data is still sparse and not fully consistent (e.g. the Cochrane Collaboration 2009). It can be a challenge to engage children in exercise, especially those who may have motor difficulties to begin with. They may not be able to access community or school recreational activities due to physical limitations or behavioral difficulties, or they may simply not enjoy exercise, sports, and other physical activities. However, there are increasingly community-based programs to foster physical activity in unique ways that are engaging for children with a range of special needs, both inclusive and specialized programs. We recommend the following general strategies:

— Capitalize on the child's interests and strengths. A child who loves music will be much more likely to participate in a dance-based activity. Dance videos and other movement games, systems, and apps are becoming increasingly popular and readily available. More and more gyms offer workout equipment, such as treadmills and elliptical machines, that come with a variety of video options, including game levels that are connected to the activity.

— Incorporate favorite family members, friends, or therapists into the activity. Going swimming with the kids next door or with cousins may be much more motivating than signing up for private lessons with a swim instructor.

— Integrate exercise into typical community or group experiences so it is consistently built into the child's day. Programs such as BOKS reflect this kind of effort (see www. bokskids.org/about-boks).

— Collaborate across school and home to prioritize physical activity by setting goals and scheduling regular exercise times. Since improved fitness can affect academic success as well as physical and emotional well-being in some children (e.g. Hilton *et al.* 2014), physical activity and fitness goals can be incorporated into the child's individualized education plan (IEP) if anxiety is impacting a child's ability to access aspects of school life.

3. General well-being

This may be harder to define and identify than problems with sleep or physical activity and more complicated to address, but it is equally important. Working to ensure that a child's situation at home and at school is healthy, safe, and strong and is a match for their needs contributes to bringing their baseline anxiety to the lowest level possible. Children who are having social and academic successes, who feel they have choices and some control over their lives, and who feel understood and supported by family and school staff are likely to experience a lower baseline anxiety level than when these factors are not in place. When life at home or at school is problematic for one or more reasons, it tends to affect all aspects of life.

Consider this typical scenario: A child who was happy and successful in elementary school for five years and then transitions to middle school has a lot to deal with: a new building in a new part of town, all new teachers who don't know him, larger classes and a busier, more stimulating, and more socially demanding environment, and a whole new peer group. The family notices the child is once again afraid of the dark and has trouble separating. Although he got over his fear of loud noises, this is also resurfacing. While targeting the specific fears is helpful, addressing the bigger problem, that of making the entire middle school experience more manageable, will help reduce baseline anxiety and may also reduce the fears that resurfaced.

4. Relaxation/sensory diet

Teaching and regularly practicing relaxation strategies and exercises throughout the day can reduce baseline anxiety in children with and without developmental disabilities. Identifying the kinds of activities, when and how to use them can be accomplished by parents and teachers in conjunction with an occupational therapist and/or mental health specialist. While activities such as yoga, T'ai Chi or taking a brisk walk may be relaxing for some, they may cause increased stress for others, or they may be inaccessible due to cognitive or physical limitations. It is crucial that the exercises and routines be highly individualized and tailored to the child's needs, abilities, and preferences.

5. Mindfulness

This is the practice of focusing one's attention on emotions, thoughts, and sensations in a non-judgmental way, not dwelling on them, and staying mentally present in the moment, and it can help some children. There are increasingly encouraging findings regarding the positive impact of this practice on baseline anxiety in the general population (Davis and Hayes 2011), and more tools and techniques are being developed to make these strategies accessible to children (e.g. Salzman and Santorelli 2014) including specifically children with high functioning autism/Asperger's (e.g. Moog and McHenry 2014). While some mindfulness materials and strategies require higher levels of language, social, and reflective capacities than many children with ASD have, there are some materials some children can access with adult instruction and support. More and more electronic apps and video products related to meditation, mindfulness, and relaxation are being produced and we anticipate in the future there will be increasing accessible materials requiring less language skills.

6. Social engagement

Connecting and engaging socially and sharing positive affect contributes to overall well-being, according to numerous studies across disciplines. We have written elsewhere about the concept of a social-affective diet (Levine, Chedd and Bauch 2009), that discusses making sure not only that the child's physical arousal/regulation systems are attended to, but also their social systems. Because children with ASD and other developmental challenges are generally less successful at accessing peer interaction, they are often far less socially engaged for far more time during the school day than their typical peers. We know from adult research that regular social engagement reduces anxiety (Umberson and Montez 2010) and recent research with animals demonstrates the extreme, unhealthy impact of negative social interactions, especially bullying (Cryan and Holmes 2005). Children with ASD are at an even greater risk than their typical peers for being bullied, which often results in increased anxiety and depression. Social isolation has also been repeatedly found to be linked to many negative outcomes related to increased physical, emotional, and behavioral challenges (Cohen 2004; Thoits 2011). Maximizing regular, pleasurable, social engagement throughout the school day and at home can reduce baseline anxiety in many children.

CHAPTER 2
OVERVIEW OF PHOBIA TREATMENT

I've developed a new philosophy.
I only dread one day at a time.
CHARLIE BROWN

This chapter discusses the general approaches and principles common to phobia treatments for typically developing children and children with ASD and introduces the components of our four-step model in this context.

How do adults, parents, and teachers tend to naturally treat their children's fears?

Some phobia triggers simply can be worked around or even avoided completely, and sometimes this is the most reasonable solution. For example, a young child afraid of the noisy, busy school cafeteria and repelled by its funny smells, shuts down throughout lunch and remains withdrawn and emotionally fragile for the rest of the school day. While it might be possible, even preferable, eventually, to implement this four-step model gradually and thoughtfully in order to help this child reach a point of not panicking in the cafeteria, his lunchtime may be better spent with a few classmates in a quieter, calmer, social setting, such as a "lunch bunch." Instead of becoming emotionally depleted, he could leave lunch each day emotionally rejuvenated, having had successful interactions with peers.

For many phobia triggers, however, avoidance is not an option—medical and dental appointments, for example. For others, avoidance decreases a child's opportunity for fun, growth, and well-being. Families of children with many phobias are also affected in negative ways. They find their worlds getting smaller and smaller as they avoid an ever-expanding list of trigger situations and activities. So treating these phobias becomes important for quality of life, not only of the child but of the rest of the family as well.

Reassurance is not always reassuring

Often adults reassure children, thinking this will help them cope ("You'll be fine! Don't worry!" or "Relax. Forget about that noise"). While this might work for small issues, in general if a few simple, comforting words significantly lessen the fear, the child did not have an actual phobia, which is good news. But imagine this scenario: You have an intense fear of flying, are on the plane, which is on the runway, ready for take-off, and you are beginning to panic. The person in the next seat says "Don't worry. You'll be fine." This could be annoying ("You just don't get it, do you?!"), or confusing ("I'm obviously not fine at all!"), or the message might not register at all. Sometimes children who do feel better briefly in response to adult reassurance, but not enough to overcome the horrible, persistent feelings from the phobia, will request more and more reassurance, and this can have the opposite effect leading to more anxiety about not getting sufficient reassurance. It can, in fact, intensify the negative adult–child interactions as well as amplify the distress experience for the child.

Good intentions don't always lead to good results
Another typical, well-intended adult approach is misrepresenting the feared event, minimizing the real possibility that the incident the child is afraid of will occur. That is, a parent may reassure an anxious child afraid of making mistakes: "You're really smart. You'll do just fine." Or a nurse may tell a patient who is about to get a shot, "Don't worry; this won't hurt a bit." Although well-intentioned, not telling the truth about a situation that is known to cause anxiety and perhaps pain, may compromise a trusting relationship between the adult and child and set up a very negative dynamic that may be difficult to repair.

Another approach that caregivers employ is refraining from telling the child in advance about an upcoming event that has triggered a major fear response in the past in an effort to avoid the often debilitating anticipatory anxiety. Unfortunately, this does not usually diminish the child's extreme reaction during the actual event and he will continue to experience the same level of fear when the event occurs. Or it may result in the child becoming even more anxious, more of the time; since he got no prior warning this time, this terrible event could happen any day, any time, and he may worry about it constantly because the possibility is always there.

Some parents and caregivers may take still another approach, especially when they feel they have tried everything else and nothing has worked. They assume that the child can and will conquer their fear if exposed to the situation or object often and/or for a prolonged time. For example, the child who is afraid of the cafeteria may continue to eat there regardless of distress, intentionally placed there by a well-meaning teacher who thinks, "She'll get used to it eventually." This approach is similar to "flooding," which is another form of exposure therapy, in which the person with a phobia is directly confronted with large amounts of the feared stimulus. Occasionally this approach can be successful, especially if the actual trigger isn't particularly distressing to the child, if the child is very motivated to succeed and please the adult, and if the child has strong coping skills already. Often parents and teachers have to put their children in situations of distress in the interim before they can work on or achieve successful treatment. For example, a child may absolutely need to have blood drawn to determine appropriate medical care before one can begin to work on or resolve their phobia of injections and needles. For some children, but especially for those with autism, who are often at a cognitive, communicative, and emotional disadvantage, approaches such as flooding as a form of treatment may induce an unmanageable level of distress and hence increase the intensity of the phobia.

Overview and brief history of phobia treatments
Cognitive, behavioral, and cognitive behavioral therapy
While there are many approaches to treating phobias in typically developing children, the most common treatment models involve a combination of teaching relaxation skills, helping the child to understand how anxiety works, and then working together with the child to develop a gradual exposure plan that will lead to increased tolerance. Cognitive behavioral therapy (CBT) with its many variations is the most common approach. CBT, not surprisingly, has its roots in both behavioral theory and therapies and cognitive theory and therapies.

Perhaps the best known and one of the earliest behavioral treatments was developed by Joseph Wolpe in the 1950s (Wolpe 1954; 1958). However, long before this, in 1924, a woman named Cover Jones wrote up her treatment, which was successful with a typical child, "Peter," for his rabbit phobia using what we would now call gradual exposure. She described placing a rabbit in closer and closer proximity to Peter, while allowing him to eat his favorite food: candy (Jones 1924). Subsequently Wolpe developed the concept he termed "reciprocal inhibition" (Wolpe 1954), which referred to his hypothesis that while experiencing an emotion incompatible with anxiety, one could not feel anxiety. That is, one cannot be anxious and not anxious at the same time. He used assertiveness training as the incompatible tool to treat people with social anxiety, the idea being that one could not be socially aggressive or angry and simultaneously be anxious.

Current behaviorists continue to use this approach, now often calling it "teaching an incompatible behavior." So a child who always runs along the illustrated train track on the "circle time" rug whenever he approaches it, might be taught to sit down as soon as he gets to the rug, as sitting is incompatible with running.

Wolpe expanded his concept of reciprocal inhibition through his discovery that assertiveness training was not effective for other types of anxiety. He developed the concept and term "systematic desensitization," which is the basis for most current anxiety treatment models, including the one presented in this book, and was also the basis for Cover Jones' earlier work. Systematic desensitization is the supposition that if one is exposed in a step-wise fashion to small, manageable but gradually increasing amounts of the phobia trigger, the fear will subside and one can then move on to tolerating more exposure. He incorporated reciprocal inhibition into this model, teaching muscle relaxation strategies for his patients to practice as they were experiencing increasing amounts of exposure to their fear, as it is less likely that people will experience anxiety while simultaneously physically relaxing.

The evolution of CBT

The cognitive aspects of cognitive behavioral therapy stemmed from the work of several psychologists, including Albert Ellis, who developed his theory of rational therapy (1957), based on the assumption that people hold mistaken beliefs and have faulty thought processes about themselves and their experiences that are counterproductive and self-destructive. His treatment was based in the process of helping people change these beliefs and thought patterns. Subsequently, Aaron Beck developed cognitive therapy, further elaborating on the model of faulty cognitive beliefs being at the root of various mental health disorders including anxiety, and the therapeutic effectiveness of helping patients change those beliefs (Beck 1970; 1976).

Commonly cited cognitive errors made by people who are prone to anxiety include believing that a threat is far greater and/or more likely to occur than it is, and that their own capacity to cope with the threat is less than it is. A person with a phobia of thunderstorms overestimates the danger and harm it could cause and underestimates their own power to cope and remain safe. Over time various ways of merging the cognitive approaches of helping people recognize and change their mistaken beliefs and self-destructive thoughts with the behaviorally-based, systematic desensitization and learning relaxation techniques came to be known as the cognitive behavioral therapies.

CBT takes many forms

In some forms of CBT people are taught to change their beliefs. In several more recent models that overtly incorporate what has come to be known as "mindfulness" approaches, such as acceptance and commitment therapy (Hayes, Follette and Linehan 2011), people are taught to notice and accept their feelings, including those that are distorted and unpleasant, and to change their feelings towards these thoughts and beliefs, rather than trying to change the thoughts themselves. In these models, people learn to be aware of and acknowledge undesirable thoughts and feelings (e.g. "I am starting to feel anxious" as the plane takes off), while not becoming overwhelmed and consumed by them. People are encouraged to notice the feelings as they enter their awareness, without trying to push away or otherwise react to these feelings. One can, in fact, conceptualize this as a process of gradual exposure and increasing tolerance to one's own frightening thoughts, just as one is also experiencing gradual exposure to the actual trigger event.

Recent adaptations of CBT

A number of professionals have developed materials and manuals for those treating children, using CBT techniques. Aureen Pinto Wagner has created particularly comprehensive CBT materials especially geared to working with children, including guides for teachers, parents, therapists, and even a book written expressly for children: *Up and Down the Worry Hill* (Wagner 2013). These materials can be found at the Lighthouse Press website www.lighthouse-press.com. "*Coping Cat*" (Kendal and Hedtke 2006) is a manualized cognitive behavior therapy package for typically developing children ages 6 to 17 that has also proven effective in various forms for many. In a very recent version of this treatment paradigm, phobias were successfully treated in high-functioning school-aged children with ASD through gradual exposure via virtual reality in combination with teaching cognitive restructuring and relaxation techniques (Maskey *et al.* 2014).

CBT and autism

There have been several recent studies finding success for children with high functioning autism/Asperger's, using adaptations of CBT (e.g. Lang *et al.* 2010; Sukhodolsky *et al.* 2013). Adaptations often include adding behavioral elements such as differential reinforcers, which is the process of positively responding to/reinforcing desirable behaviors and not responding at all to undesirable ones, and systematic prompting, another technique for increasing appropriate behaviors, sometimes referred to as "errorless learning." In the most recent review, most of the studies included children ages seven through adolescence with an IQ of at least 70. Hence, young children, and/or children with more significant social and cognitive impairment were not included. No studies using CBT with more impacted children have been found, likely because the "C" (Cognitive) components of CBT are generally oriented towards the higher levels of language, and the more skilled social interaction which are needed as the child and therapist talk, plan, and review collaboratively. Another requirement is the capacity to discuss, plan and report one's internal thought processes and experiences, i.e. meta-cognitive awareness.

Emphasis on behavioral components

Most studies and guides for treating phobias in children with ASD or other developmental disabilities, aside from the highest functioning group, primarily use the behavioral components of phobia treatments. That is, they incorporate earlier approaches, such as systematic desensitization, now generally called gradual exposure.

The typical treatment paradigm—with variations—of phobias in children with autism/and intellectual disability involves gradual exposure combined with and/or rewarded by a tangible, desirable item (Jennett and Hagopian 2008). Like CBT, this model involves gradually increasing exposure to the feared event. However, unlike CBT, the exposure hierarchy is constructed by the adult. Preferred items are based on observation or experimentation and then are paired with increasing exposure. In most studies, instead of children learning and practicing relaxation strategies, they are given preferred items, either as a distraction or as a reward for tolerating more and more of the targeted fear, or both. The child afraid of a needle injection, for example, is given favorite snacks or toys while tolerating closer proximity/longer physical contact with a needle.

Some paradigms incorporate "escape prevention" and "forced exposure," during which the child is prevented from stopping before the hierarchy dictates, regardless of distress, while others stop exposure when the child exits and restart it again later. This paradigm is generally successful over time since the child gradually becomes more able to tolerate the trigger.

In this more traditional treatment model for children with ASD, however, children often initially experience significant distress when the exposure level increases, even by small amounts, i.e. when they are exposed to increasing approximations of the feared object or situation, until they become used to it. Further, in this model, unlike in CBT, children aren't taught self-regulating strategies such as relaxation, or co-regulating strategies (e.g. doing something enjoyable with the adult) to decrease anxiety. Finally, another objection to this model is that it may be experienced as coercive, with the adult inducing distress to the child, albeit in the interest of ultimately reducing child distress. This is in great contrast to CBT, which is a highly collaborative process between child and therapist, or often between child, parents, and therapist. (See Figures 2.1 and 2.2.)

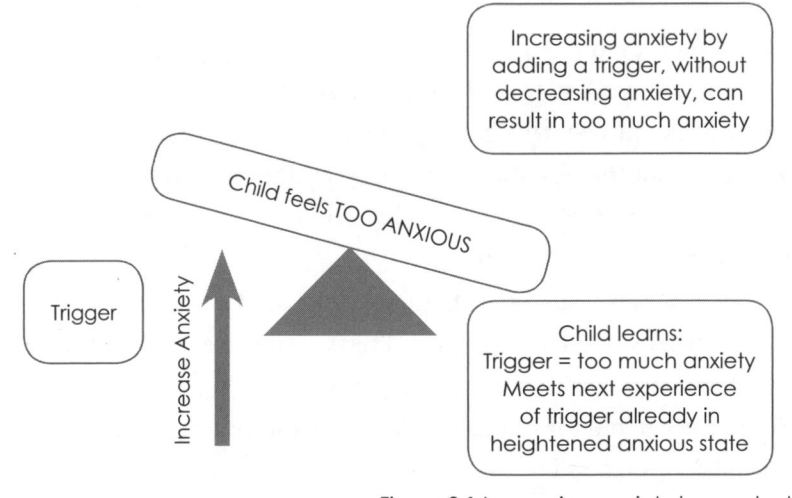

Figure 2.1 Increasing anxiety by gradual exposure, without decreasing anxiety.

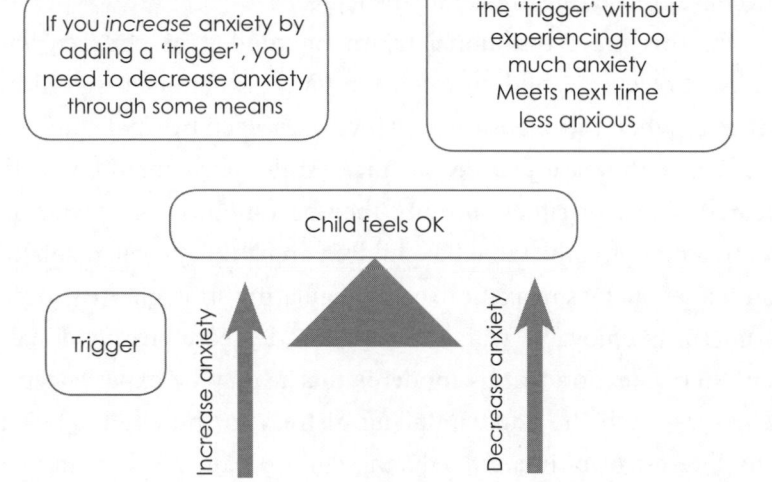

Figure 2.2 Increasing anxiety by gradual exposure while adding measures to decrease anxiety.

Play therapy

There is a long history of play therapy with young children, using pretend and symbolism to help children act out their emotions and experiences in order to gain mastery over them. Much has been written about therapeutically helping children use symbolic play to conquer their emotions, especially around exposure to traumatic situations (Gil and Terr 2013).

Play therapy isn't often the treatment used with children with ASD, perhaps because limited and restricted pretend play is part of the diagnostic difficulty for children with this disorder (DSM-5). Some treatments for children with ASD and other developmental disabilities, such as DIR/Floortime® involve working with the child in developing meaningful symbolic play as part of supporting their overall development.

In the model we are putting forward we often use role play, video or visual representation, and pretend play integrated into gradual exposure for children who can make the connection between symbolic and the actual phobia trigger. In our clinical experience, children who don't spontaneously engage in pretend play often do understand and participate in brief pretend elements that are closely related to their own phobic experiences.

A child who doesn't naturally pretend but is terrified of bugs may recognize something very familiar or even join in when you push a plastic toy bug off your leg and stomp on it, or brush it off the leg of a realistic looking doll. It may be that a symbolic but fairly realistic and close approximation of a child's actual, intense experience may be easier to understand than typical, spontaneous, and rapidly changing pretend play routines. It may also be that children can grasp some pretend scenarios "receptively," especially those that are highly emotionally salient to them, before they can spontaneously generate solitary or collaborative pretend "expressively."

We look forward to researchers further exploring these clinical observations. Not all children with ASD or other developmental disabilities are able to understand pretend, even in this context. However, it is not necessary to recognize or identify with all the components in order to benefit from the model we describe.

CHAPTER 3
GRADUAL EXPOSURE, HUMOR, AND INTERACTIVE PLAY

Common sense and a sense of humor are the
same thing, moving at different speeds. A sense
of humor is just common sense, dancing.
WILLIAM JAMES

How our model is similar to and different from others

In the model we are putting forward in this book, the same principles of gradual exposure paired with measures to reduce child distress that are a cornerstone of behavioral approaches and cognitive behavioral approaches, are incorporated. These tools are common to CBT and the gradual exposure paradigm typically used with children with ASD, and they have a very strong evidence base. However, in our model, the process is highly individualized and collaborative: self and co-regulating strategies specific to the child are designed and implemented in order to actively reduce anxiety, as one increases the anxiety by exposures.

Self-regulating strategies, such as listening to favorite music, as well as co-regulating strategies such as interactive, playful humor are integrated. Exposure to greater levels of the fearful event are based solely on the child's emotional responses, such that distress is not induced. While the child is experiencing closer approximations of what scares them, they are also experiencing an enjoyable activity and/or interaction that simultaneously lowers their anxiety.

Our model also incorporates gradual exposure to fearful feelings and fearful responding. The adult demonstrates experiences of mild fear within the context of gradual exposure, but in a modified, playful version that is manipulated to be of interest to, and is also often funny to the child. For example, the adult playfully acts out experiencing small amounts of fear, which is under the control of the child. That is, the child can push the "start button" for the sound of thunder and the adult can covers their ears, exaggerate a grimace, and yell or pantomime "STOP!" with a knowing smile. This is perhaps most similar to the mindfulness component in CBT therapy models such as acceptance and commitment therapy (ACT), as it acknowledges the fearful feelings while trying to create a new association with the source of fear.

Fear, itself

In our model the child's fearful responses to the real trigger, their fearful feelings, are not avoided, ignored, or minimized by the adult. Rather, they are explicitly included in playful re-enactments, just as in mindfulness/ACT in which the person experiencing a fearful or anxiety-provoking thought learns to experience that thought or feeling, but without becoming overwhelmed by it by changing their response to the feeling—their "feeling about the feeling." We don't know yet if this component is indeed an "active ingredient" in this treatment model; we'll continue to explore this hypothesis as well as leave it to researchers to determine over time. However, we do have the impression from our clinical experience that it is this part of the process that especially captures children's attention and engages them emotionally. It is often during this part of the process that they are able to tolerate increasing the gradual exposure.

We also see that parents who have repeatedly experienced their child's phobic response and have had to deal with a very distressed child, sometimes multiple times on a daily basis, have, understandably, developed their own intense emotional responses to the anticipation of the trigger. When they are able to do it, they often find this kind of play to be a great relief. Perhaps it also helps them to develop new patterns of emotional responding that, in turn, helps the child respond differently too.

Using humor

Humor is a very serious subject. Throughout our work and in our examples we make extensive use of humor. We work to get children in a relaxed, playful mood before we tackle their fears or directly approach what makes them anxious. With most children (and adults too), we infuse our actual sessions with lightness and humor, although never diminishing or dismissing their very real, very distressing feelings and responses. We do this carefully and thoughtfully, with the following tenets in mind:

— Socially sharing humor can greatly reduce anxiety (Gaberson 1995). When there is turbulence on an airplane flight, an unusual sound or movement in an elevator or an unexpected or dramatic occurrence in a crowded place, it is not unusual to notice people making spontaneous jokes or sharing knowing facial expressions, all in an effort to connect with others who are probably anxious and uncomfortable too. This often decreases everyone's anxiety. Humor and especially laughter create bonds among people, even in frightening situations. It may even have some lasting health benefits (Lovorn 2008; Schacht and Stewart 1990). Laughing together and sharing an experience with others about components of one's fear relieves tension, even temporarily, from unpleasant feelings. And sometimes the relief is permanent.

— Sharing laughter and infusing humor can help a child tolerate increasing exposure to the phobia trigger. In many of our examples, children are in a socially engaged, playful state and are truly enjoying themselves as we gradually increase the exposure to their phobia. Five-year-old Will (see Chapter 5) finds it hilarious to watch the video of his brother hamming it up in response to toilets flushing and hand dryers blowing loudly, the very sounds he finds so disturbing in the real world. An eight-year-old we worked with who "needed" to cough an even number of times started laughing as he ordered his Spiderman action figure to cough an odd number of times. Another patient who used to scream and cover her ears whenever someone sang "Happy Birthday" learned to tolerate it when singing "Happy Birthday" to the toaster and her cat.

— Many young children find it very entertaining to watch adults playfully pretending to be afraid of the very thing that they, themselves, are afraid of. It can reduce their fear response through increasing their exposure, but in a safe, non-threatening, and amusing way.

Grown-ups behaving badly

Interestingly and happily, the very dynamic of engaging with a child in this way around their phobias, during which the child is in control of the length and magnitude of the adult's playful version of distress, is often very funny to children, with or without disabilities. We are not sure why. Is the child experiencing a high degree of relief from being in charge of the response that controls them and takes over their sense of safety and well-being? Is it the juxtaposition of the all-powerful, brave adult figure, pretending to be afraid of what the child knows is only their own, that the adult shouldn't be scared of their silly or childish fear? Or is it that when the adult exaggerates a fear response, it is no longer scary but totally ridiculous and entertaining? We don't really know, but have observed children of all ages, adolescents, and even adults involved in this kind of play, countless times, engaged in fully pleasurable, deep laughter, the kind that is contagious and spreads to all those around them.

Even without fully understanding why a child finds these adult re-enactments funny, the fact that they do allows the adult to increase the exposure to the real phobia with the child sustaining a happy state—and this is a major and necessary component in reducing the impact of the feared object or experience, sometimes even permanently extinguishing the phobia.

What about children for whom this kind of play is not funny?

Or what about children who don't seem to find humor in anything?

There is a great range of temperaments and personalities, and some children simply have a flat or more serious temperament. It may be difficult or even impossible to use humor in their treatment. For these children, other strategies that decrease anxiety are likely to be more effective. However, in our experience it is quite rare to find a child who will not laugh at something. But it can take a lot of experimentation and the willingness to try a lot of subjects, styles, and variations.

Too close for comfort?

Sometimes, if the child does not appear to find humor in all the toy play and routines that typically work, they may be experiencing too much anxiety to relax enough to have a good laugh. The subject or story may be too close for comfort, too real, and trigger a fear response. They may be extremely fearful of losing control and perhaps causing the very situation that scares them to occur. One child who was extremely afraid of spiders, which is very common, wouldn't even say the word, "spider," because she thought it would make them instantly appear. A combination of spelling, singing, whispering, and befriending some "virtual" spiders on her laptop helped her tolerate both saying and looking at spiders, at least from a distance.

Working with the child's educational or treatment team and family to explore when, where, and how the child experiences enjoyment and social humor will be key in most successful treatment plans. We had a patient who was serious, afraid or angry—or all three—almost all the time and about a variety of things. However, he loved being tickled and would become more relaxed and happy for a while during and after a tickling session. He especially enjoyed when his father and little sister tickled him together. So we supported incorporating social tickling play sessions with his father and sister into the gradual exposure process.

Not just for kids

Sometimes older children, especially those in or approaching the middle school years, may feel that such playfulness is silly and "babyish" or just plain embarrassing. And it might draw more attention to their fear and heighten their self-consciousness. For some, however, once they intellectually understand how it can be part of the treatment and may help them, and they get more familiar and comfortable with this approach, they may be more willing to engage. But for others, silly, exaggerated play simply is not an effective part of the treatment.

When not to tease

Never, ever give the impression that you are laughing at or making fun of the child or dismissing their fears as foolish or insignificant. It is sometimes difficult but absolutely critical to make sure the child feels you are on their side, that you are working with them against the fear, and not laughing at them or intentionally trying to make them feel foolish or more fearful. Playfully acting out the child's fear response but overdoing it may be funny to some but not to others, as they may interpret it as mean-spirited teasing or mocking them. So knowing the child well, closely monitoring their responses, as well as the pace and magnitude of the playful re-enactments and then making adjustments in style, tone, language and actions are the best ways to avoid this misinterpretation.

Making many understanding comments and checking in with the child while one is going through the playful re-enactment helps frame the scenario in a safe, supportive, empathic laughing-with-and-not-laughing-at context (e.g. "But the thunder is TOO LOUD for ME!"; "That shot is going to HURT HURT HURT!"). On the other hand, avoid making comments that diminish the validity of the child's fear, such as saying, "See? There's nothing to be afraid of. You were silly to worry about that," or "You don't need to cry. Spiderman didn't cry, right?" This might be experienced as shaming or insulting to the child.

Nobody is perfect

If one does make a mistake, if the child responds with increased fear, sadness or hurt feelings, immediately apologize and work toward repairing the situation. Let the child know that adults make mistakes too, sometimes very big mistakes, and that was one of them. Maybe even add some humor: say you were "a real dummy" or "a Big Bozo" and really mean it. Or just say you blew it and move on, take a different approach, use a different tone.

Using humor in treating fears and phobias, or using humor in any therapeutic intervention needs to be taken very seriously and handled with extreme skill, care, and sensitivity. If executed correctly, it can often be tremendously fun and effective, not only in reducing the fear response, but also in further strengthening the bond between adult and child and setting the stage for more enjoyable interactions and time spent together in the future.

Incorporating interactive play

Engaging in play of any kind but especially interactive play with a trusted adult involving familiar topics, even those that make a child anxious or uncomfortable, can, in addition to providing a medium for gradual exposure to the object or event, also do the following:

— Enhances and strengthens the relationship between the child and parent, caregiver, teacher or therapist. It is a way of communicating. The adult is saying, in effect, "I understand how you are feeling. That feeling is an understandable feeling. We're tackling this together." This is especially true for nonverbal children or those with very limited language who enjoy playing, with whom one can't use language to express this complex, empathic supportive stance.

— Increases feelings of safety and security. Even when playing out the child's most stressful experiences, doing so interactively with a trusted adult who monitors the child's response, adjusting the play accordingly to keep it engaging but not scary can greatly increase the child's experience of comfort and well-being.

— Increases the child's ability to express him/herself, rather than inhibit expression of thoughts and feelings, thereby diminishing their power. Rather than telling the child to forget about what's bothering him/her, the adult is respectfully helping the child express their initially intense and overwhelming thoughts, feelings, and experiences.

— Helps the child to reframe/redefine the feared object or event and see it in neutral or even positive terms. Through play, increased exposures, and sometimes rational explanations, the source of fear loses its power and toxicity. ("I was so scared of bees. I thought I wouldn't be able to stand it if I got stung. A sting would hurt but I would be OK. I still don't like them but they can't freak me out.")

— Promotes a sense of control, sometimes symbolically and sometimes in reality, in a child who feels no sense of control over what has or will happen as related to the phobia.

— Increases self-confidence. ("I did it!")

Implementing the treatment approach described in the next seven chapters with children with autism and related disorders may prove successful. It is true that the actual event may continue to be unpleasant. But the anticipatory anxiety associated with it can often be dramatically reduced, and the degree and duration of anxiety experienced during the event can often be decreased as well. In other words, while injections still hurt; loud noises startle; and losing is less fun than winning, these experiences can become more tolerable and manageable for children. And their negative impact on the entire family, on classmates and teammates and on other important people in the child's life may be considerably reduced.

CHAPTER 4

FOUR-STEP TREATMENT MODEL

This chapter provides a description of the four-step treatment model. This model is based on the evidence-based principles of gradual exposures combined with strategies to decrease anxiety. Highly individualizing both the gradual exposure process and the anxiety-decreasing range of strategies as well as closely monitoring the child's responses and adjusting accordingly are its unique components. Steps 1–3 are preparation phases, while Step 4 is the actual desensitizing process, which incorporates the information and tools developed in the first three steps.

Step 1. Identify key trigger components of the feared object or situation: "Unbundle" the phobia

Phobias generally have multiple components that vary from child to child. For example, a phobia around having injections may also include fear of going to the doctor's office, fear of medical equipment, latex gloves, tourniquet, aversion to certain odors, fear of confinement in the chair and/or anticipating being afraid—or fear of fear. One can't always know all the components or their magnitude, but figuring out some of them allows one to work to desensitize the child to each separately as well as together, which is the ultimate goal. It is much easier and less stressful to the child to work on desensitizing to distinct components, such as latex gloves, rather than to the entire anxiety-provoking experience all at once.

Fear of fear

Fear of fear, as previously mentioned, is the anticipation of the fear as the trigger approaches, as one tells the child the trigger will approach, or as the child sees evidence of what comes before the trigger is starting to happen, and/or the first mild feeling of fear. It is perhaps universal in predictable phobias. Hence we almost always incorporate this as one of the elements to work on in the unbundling process.

Fear of fear can be effectively incorporated into working on each component in the bundle, as well as each level of exposure to each component. That is, the adult can pretend to be afraid, startled or upset in response to any of the elements at any level. For example, the adult pretends to be afraid when the child approaches him with the pretend syringe or pretends to hold their nose with playfully exaggerated disgust when child holds up the alcohol wipe. The adult can incorporate exposure to small amounts of the fear experiences in many different ways, depending on what pretence of fear is appealing (and probably funny, and not at all scary or threatening to the specific child around the specific event at that specific time). This re-enactment can involve playful, slapstick pretend, may involve physical humor (pretending to fall down with fear when child approaches the adult with a small stuffed dog), or playful, humorous language (the adult says he will never come back to the doctor, "Never ever, not in a million years!"; or she says she will "Tear that hard math assignment into a gazillion pieces!"), or exaggerating the horrified rejection of the feared object. (The adult pretends to throw the feared item or symbolic representation of it out the window or into the trash.)

It is key to observe the child closely to determine if your playful exaggeration is striking a familiar chord and is compelling, interesting and/or funny. Sometimes what is funny one day will be scary or uninteresting the next, depending on the child's state. We worked with a child who, when his brother participated in the initial session, found all sorts of playful fear exaggeration hilarious, as did his (non-fearful) brother, and we were able to make great headway. At the next session, however, his mother brought him without his brother, and the initial attempt at humor was not as successful. He seemed more anxious, did not find the same things funny, and remained flat and frightened until we engaged him in playing kickball, a favorite activity, which reduced his anxiety and got him to a more playful baseline state.

Why unbundle phobias?

Why not just use gradual exposure for small amounts of the whole trigger event?

Unbundling a phobia, working on the child becoming comfortable with smaller components of the trigger event, is generally much easier, both for the child and the adult, than working on the child tolerating small amounts of the whole event.

We consulted with a school where a child was afraid to go into the cafeteria at lunchtime. The school had developed a gradual exposure plan in which the child was to go into the cafeteria for one, then two, then three minutes, and so on, while holding a favorite toy. This plan, while also based in gradual exposure, was not successful; even entering the cafeteria at lunchtime for a single minute consistently caused the child to scream and try to bolt. The educational team wasn't sure which aspect of the cafeteria was upsetting, although they suspected it might be a combination of the noise level, crowded tables, smells of food cooking, and the child's low interest in eating in general.

Once they closely analyzed the experience, the team was able to work on small manageable components separately. That is, they unbundled working on the going-in-the-cafeteria-at-lunchtime into (1) being in the cafeteria (with a favorite adult doing a favorite activity) during mid-morning when the cafeteria was empty; (2) eating in the cafeteria in mid-morning without other students present; (3) going to an all-school assembly in the cafeteria when food wasn't present; (4) going in the cafeteria just before lunch when smells from the kitchen were present; and (5) ensuring the child's own lunch included highly preferred foods. Over time, once they had worked to get the child comfortable with each component they were able to work towards the entire going-in-the-cafeteria-at-lunchtime experience much more effectively.

While older children who are verbal and articulate may be able to explain exactly what it is about the trigger that is distressing, many children with developmental challenges are not able to describe their fears. Additionally, even for older more verbal children, the whole "black cloud" of the trigger experience may be undifferentiated; the intense, negative emotions experienced by just thinking about it may make it impossible for the child to separate out various components. They cannot identify what is tolerable and what is distressing. Finally, it is common for phobias to spread to related objects and events, which also become triggers. So whatever initially caused the distress may not be as important to determine. All components have to be targeted.

How do you unbundle an experience when you don't know what is upsetting or why?

Sometimes it is clear which components in a trigger are upsetting to a child. For example, children may exhibit patterns of several phobia triggers with similar properties, such as loud sudden sounds. So if a child is afraid of sirens, vacuum cleaners, thunder, and fire alarms, one or more aspects of the sound component is frightening, or was at one time. But there may be additional components that can be further unbundled, including the unpredictability of the sound or the perceived danger or emergency aspect, and these are also contributing to the child's fear and can be worked on separately. In our experience, unbundling what appear to be fairly straightforward phobias makes the process more tolerable and more fun.

Sometimes it is difficult to know what exactly is frightening to the child. We treated a child with a fear of butterflies. Whenever he saw one he would bolt, sometimes into a parking lot or busy street. We didn't know which components might be contributing to this fear so we unbundled in several ways: showing him videos, first of smiling cartoon butterflies, then of real butterflies in slow motion so he could see their movement pattern, then of happy children raising butterflies from larvae. We gave him an "app" detailing this process so he could watch it over and over. Then we introduced toy plastic butterflies into his play.

We also wondered if the sudden, unexpected moving visual stimulus was contributing to his alarm, so we created "butterfly-like" bits of wadded tissue, throwing them at each other in playful battles. Then we did this with paper cut-out butterflies and then with the small plastic butterflies.

Leave no stone unturned

While proceeding through this process, one often discovers that specific components that didn't seem distressing to the child initially are in fact, "the culprits." We were working with a child who was afraid of getting many different substances on his hands—common snacks, sandwich fillings, pudding and other foods, art materials like glue, Play-Doh, and glitter, dirt, sand, and the list goes on. This grew into a full-blown contamination fear of touching someone or something that had come in contact with one of these substances. Understandably, this fear was having a major, negative impact on his family and school life.

Our initial unbundling focused on the appearance, smell, and texture of these materials. Our patient became increasingly more tolerant as we worked through them, one by one. He began, touching some that he previously avoided and even used several for more extensive periods—gluing plastic shapes on paper, for example. However, he continued to fear others, including toast, sugary foods and glitter. One day he calmly and comfortably scattered glitter on paper, and we thought perhaps he conquered his fear. But soon he began to panic as he struggled unsuccessfully to get the glitter off his hand, with sparkles still evident after repeated rubbing. He calmed down only when we were able to wash it off entirely.

Based on this experience (and others like it), we realized that worrying that he wouldn't be able to remove substances from his hands was an element in the fear bundle. Sugar sprinkles, tiny toast crumbs, and glitter can become lodged in sweaty, sticky little palms! So we proceeded to work specifically on removing a range of "stuff," from larger bits that were easier to tolerate to smaller, stickier, more disturbing ones, from his and our hands. The removal component, getting crumbs and sprinkles and the like off his hands, was not a strand we had originally identified as part of his phobia.

Hitting the wall

When one runs into a wall in the gradual exposure process, the problem may be that the trigger itself is still too distressing for the child to tolerate, even in its unbundled forms. Further unbundling, although challenging, will often continue to move the process forward. One reason is that experiences that we generally think of as whole experiences are actually made up of several smaller or more complicated events. It may feel just like trying to further factor a prime number! We have found that this becomes easier with time, experience, and the willingness to experiment with very slight variations. We have provided an Appendix with some unbundling approaches we have used for some of the more common phobias (see Appendix).

Here are the general guidelines for unbundling:

1. SEPARATING OUT THE VARIOUS SENSORY COMPONENTS

— visual

— tactile

— auditory

— olfactory

Many experiences that may have been disturbing initially because of just one component have other sensory components embedded that have also become frightening, perhaps by association. For example, the smell of alcohol wipes often involves getting a shot. The sight of a dark, cloudy sky may mean a thunderstorm is imminent. Hearing the bathtub filling up means a hairwash is sure to follow.

2. SEPARATING OUT THE ACTUAL STIMULUS FROM THE SUDDEN UNEXPECTED SURPRISE COMPONENT

This is easiest to conceptualize with sound-related fears. Sensitizing to the tenor and volume of thunder, a fire alarm or siren can be practiced separately from learning to tolerate the surprise element. However, the element of surprise is also connected with many other phobias and can be practiced separately from tolerating the trigger in a less sudden, more predictable form, such as seeing and eventually petting a calm dog in its crate vs. unexpectedly seeing a barking dog bounding out of a car at the playground.

3. INCLUDING THE EMOTION OF FEAR AS A COMPONENT

Anticipatory anxiety is very often key to address in the desensitization process. With more verbal and communicative children, one can often identify their anticipatory fear. For example, a child may tell his teacher, "It's almost noon, and that's when the bell rings. It scares me! I have to get out of here!" However, even nonverbal children will show signs of anticipatory anxiety. A child may observe his classmates gathering up their belongings, which always signals the end of the school day and the bell that heralds it—and he will grimace and cover his ears. Or he may cry or become extremely restless every time you drive past the building in which his pediatrician has an office. Tuning into both verbal and nonverbal cues will lead to working through the event, environment or object that is causing the anticipatory anxiety.

4. CONSIDER SEEMINGLY INSIGNIFICANT OR OVERLOOKED ELEMENTS WITHIN AN EXPERIENCE

Sometimes elements that seem at first to be one and the same as those one has already tackled or seem minor, almost invisible, turn out to be key. We worked with a child who feared going to the dentist, not uncommon among children—or adults! As she became increasingly more comfortable with most aspects—entering the office, tolerating the antiseptic smell, sitting in and even tilting way back in the chair, she was still afraid of adults putting anything in her mouth.

We realized this had generalized to other settings and circumstances, including being fed ice cream with a spoon, so we added the element of "adult putting items in child's mouth" and then developed an exposure ladder beginning on the bottom rung with an activity she enjoyed. First, she and her mother put sugary sprinkles on each other's faces and then picked them off and ate them. This was followed by putting the sprinkles on her lips, then tongue, then teeth, and then putting the sprinkles on a chopstick and then a spoon. From there we moved on to more dental tool-like objects and ultimately to actual dental tools.

See Figure 4.1 for an illustration of unbundling a phobia.

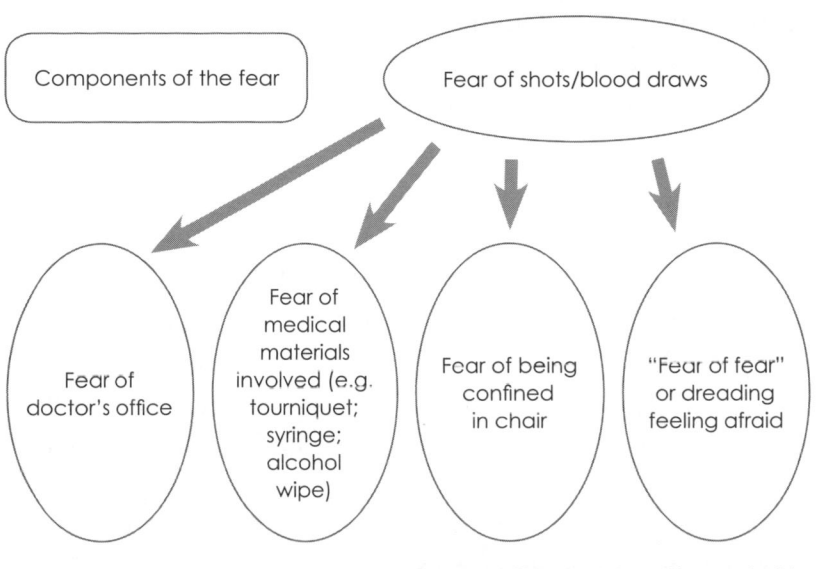

Figure 4.1 Step 1: Unbundling a phobia.

Step 2. Determine measures that reduce the child's anxiety

This step involves determining strategies that will decrease the child's distress while increasing exposure. This is the step that is generally incorporated into CBT for typically developing children, but not often used with children with ASD, particularly more impacted children. This is because it may be more challenging to decrease anxiety in a child who cannot independently and intentionally relax using visualization or engage in guided breathing exercises.

Self-regulating strategies

Specific strategies that work to decrease a child's anxiety vary from child to child. Some children with ASD are able to engage in adult-taught self-soothing strategies such as attending to breathing and specific breathing exercises, often included in CBT. Some will be able to engage in guided meditation and find this useful. We had a patient who learned T'ai Chi from watching YouTube videos and found this relaxing.

For many children with ASD, the adults can glean strategies that are self-soothing from watching what a child does that relaxes him. For example, some children are much more relaxed after running around outside or jumping on a trampoline, swinging, or dancing to rhythmic music. Incorporating these activities into work on gradual exposure, either doing them before or during the gradual exposure activities, can help keep anxiety at a manageable level. Occupational therapists (OTs) are often very helpful at coming up with activities that are regulating and soothing for specific children.

Co-regulating strategies

For many children, engaging with an adult—interacting, cuddling, laughing, playing—is especially helpful to reduce anxiety. The most effective soothing activities for typically developing children and children with developmental disabilities often involve doing something with their favorite people. In our model we make extensive use of co-regulating activities, especially playful fun activities, as tools to reduce a child's anxiety and increase their enjoyment of the work targeting their phobias. What is fun, calming and enjoyable is highly individualized, and it is key to know the child you are working with or treating, so you are able to incorporate self and co-regulating strategies that are most likely to be effective.

Step 3. Design levels of gradually increasing exposure to each component

This is what is sometimes called a "fear ladder" of steps that increasingly approximate the real trigger, or in this model, that gradually approximate the element of the unbundled trigger one is working on at first, and then the actual trigger. That is, if one is working on helping the child tolerate the sound of thunder separate from the surprise element, one could play recordings of thunder very quietly in the background while playing the child's favorite song in the foreground, using a computer, phone or both, and then gradually turning up the volume on the thunder, with ample warning ("Ready … set … here it comes…"). The adult can work with the child, or better, the child can take control of the volume while the adult monitors the child's reaction, adding guidance and encouragement or dialing down the volume if necessary.

Separate from or incorporated into this activity, the adult can tackle the surprise element, with the volume again very low, making it into a game: "When is it going to start? I don't hear it? Do you? Oh … I think … maybe … now?" One can also trade roles, and the child can "surprise" the adult, who can playfully exaggerate surprise and distress and simultaneously increase exposure to the "fear of fear" element.

Websites featuring virtually every sound and its variations can also be incorporated into other games or activities the child enjoys. For instance a child we worked with was scared of the sound of crying babies. She also loved physical clowning around, especially wobbling and falling down. So we pretended to fall down and simultaneously played a crying baby recording at a very low volume. Websites that sell sound effects for movies often have an endless number and broad range of sound effects, ideal for this purpose.

Technology and creating steps of exposure

Many new ways of using technology for these steps are highlighted. For example, there are now many electronic "apps" that incorporate exposure to common fears, such as games involving touching moving photographs of bugs and incorporating many common household sounds. Video games and apps that provide both enjoyment and exposure to specific components of the trigger experience are ideal for the desensitizing process. We anticipate that apps will become even easier to access, individualize, and personalize, making them more accessible in treating a very broad range of phobias.

There are many public access videos posted on Youtube and Vimeo that include different versions of common phobias, like thunderstorms, medical appointments, bugs (especially spiders), riding on elevators and escalators, emergency vehicles, buses and subways, through tunnels and over bridges.

It has also become very easy to make videos for this purpose, using a phone camera or similar device. Parents can record a family member or themselves engaging in the feared experience, such as having blood drawn, hearing the school bell or riding an escalator, and "hamming it up" with exaggerated affect and humor, so as to entertain and amuse the child. It is also easier than ever before to make videos of increasing exposure tailored to the child's interests, comfort level, and humor. For example, the novice videographer can make a two-minute video of a Spiderman or Lego minifigure, princess or Angry Bird or the child's own stuffed animal, covering its ears as a balloon pops, cowering in the corner at the sight of the dentist's drill or hiding under the bed when a dog barks. One can play it with no sound, in slow motion, or accompanied by the child's favorite music, over and over, and edit it quickly if it is too frightening or just not very interesting, tweaking it to maximize interest and hit just the right note.

Don't leave without me!

We worked with a child who had a fear of the school bus leaving without him. There were many contributing factors we unbundled and worked on separately, including watching videos of school buses and then real ones and pretending they had left without him. We also role played using toy buses, amplifying the desperate feeling of being left behind ("Oh no! It's LEAVING without us! Now we'll NEVER get to school.") We filmed ourselves missing the bus and we all watched the videos over and over, which was embarrassing for us—we'll never win any acting awards—but it clearly made an impact, as our patient proudly showed them to his family.

We have included an Appendix with some gradual exposure approaches we have used for some of the more common components of common phobias (see Appendix).

Here are several continuums we generally consider:

THE PRETEND-TO-REAL CONTINUUM

This may start with a drawing or a cut-out of the real thing, from a magazine, for example, progress to small, cartoonish toys and on to more realistic toys or other concrete representations, and then to some real elements mixed in with the toys.

Act out a scenario with toys, role playing with real people (you, the child, parents, teachers, counselor) with dolls, dollhouse furniture, toy food, animals, etc. Then introduce real objects and real people but not in the actual, anxiety-provoking situation, Begin away from the actual trigger area, moving gradually closer and manipulating other features, such as music, your own narration or actual conversations.

USES OF VIDEO CONTINUUM

There are many ways to use video and we give many examples in the case studies, but there are several ways to use them in a continuum, from least to most like the actual trigger event. These include: still photographs, online videos, original, personal videos with pretend or role play only; personal video of friends or family members engaging in the actual event, playfully exaggerating the fear element; bringing some form of video that is compelling to the child to the actual event (video of funny re-enactment of a scenario in the dentist's office), and the child watches it in the waiting room.

USES OF AUDIO CONTINUUM

For phobias that are sound-related or have auditory components, one can begin with making playful imitations of the sound. If the child thinks it's funny, add playful variations. For example, for a child afraid of the Happy Birthday song (which is surprisingly common!) one can begin by whispering "Happy Birthday" to Letter W or to the kitchen sink. To desensitize a child to loud clapping one can do silent, mimed, or one finger "tiny, quiet clapping," then move to one person clapping in time to the child walking or marching, then add more people or electronic audio of groups of people clapping, first with the volume turned down very low, and increasing as tolerated.

Step 4. Proceed through the levels described in Step 2, combined with anxiety reducing strategies from Step 3

This step shows how to engage in the actual desensitization process. Start with a fear component that is likely to be the easiest to desensitize to, so everyone can experience success as you become increasingly familiar and comfortable with the process. For a phobia about injections, it may be easiest to attack the medical equipment involved. Use the exposures from Step 2 (video clips showing the equipment; engaging in playful pretending with the child's favorite action figure, or an actual person), combined with the anxiety-reducing strategies from Step 3 (play the child's favorite music while showing the video clips; incorporate humor into play with latex gloves or other equipment).

An important and perhaps unique component of this model is that the process is guided by the child's response. The child should be interested and intrigued, attentive but not afraid. If the child shows signs of fear, go back down the fear ladder to less realistic exposures. Also consider adding measures for reducing anxiety, such as relaxation or breathing exercises, if the child can access them. If the child does not seem to be making the connection between your playful re-enactment and the real thing, add some realistic elements and familiar but non-threatening details.

There are many fun ways to highlight the fact that the child is actually in control of the exposure, and this part of the process may, itself, be funny to the child. The adult, by exaggerating their response through facial expressions, actions or words is often both reassuring and amusing to the child.

Singing is not always soothing

For example, we worked with a child who was afraid when adults sang. So we began to sing, which slightly annoyed the child, and then immediately covered our mouths, saying "Oops!" with an overly dramatic, embarrassed, clearly communicating, "I messed up." We then let another couple of notes "escape" from our mouths, stopping again when the child shot us a dirty look. Some children will think this is funny. And if so, it can be a way to increase exposures as the child continues to request the interaction again and again through facial expression and words. Other children, however, may find this annoying. How to do gradual exposure has to be very individualized based on the child's make-up and responses.

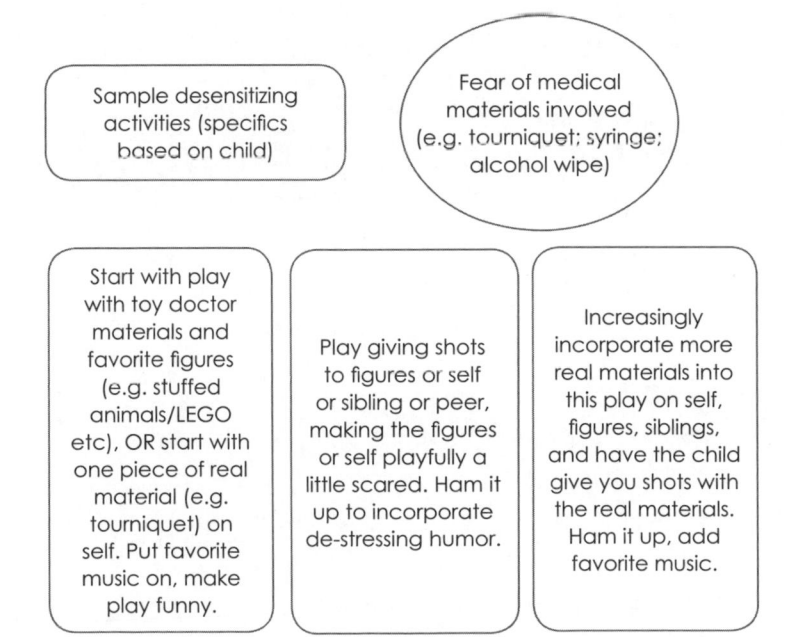

Figure 4.2 Step 4: Desensitizing to fear of the medical materials using favorite pretend figures, social humor, and favorite music to decrease anxiety.

CHAPTER 5

TREATING SOPHIA'S PHOBIA OF THUNDERSTORMS AND BUGS

> You can't depend on your eyes when
> your imagination is out of focus.
> MARK TWAIN

Background

Ever since she was a toddler, eight-year-old Sophia has had many fears. Her parents think she is happy, generally speaking, but she is a relatively serious child much of the time. Her parents notice that while many fears come and go, two have been longstanding and are interfering with life at home and at school. She is terrified of thunderstorms, and this fear has spread. She is also afraid if the sky is even a little cloudy, and she checks it constantly, peering out the window many times each day before going outside. If there is one cloud in the sky she hesitates and often returns to get her raincoat, puts it on and zips it up, including the hood, before rushing to the car. She won't participate in outdoor activities, and when the family goes to the beach, she hovers in the tent they bring along, only occasionally venturing out when her sister is doing something very appealing like building a sandcastle or collecting shells.

At school Sophia goes out at recess but rarely veers away from the building, unless the sky is completely clear and the sun is shining brightly. She checks the weather several times on the computer in the classroom and again when she gets home. When she hears about thunderstorms in other areas she becomes very concerned, especially if they are predicted to occur near her aunt and uncle or grandparents' homes, and she begs her mother to call them to make sure they are all right. Although Sophia has always had this fear, the degree to which it has spread and the intensity have worsened substantially and not coincidentally, ever since a big thunderstorm hit their town several months ago, during which a tree fell down three houses away and many others were uprooted.

What else is bugging Sophia?

Sophia's other big fear, which seems to be seasonal, is bugs. Every spring just as the weather begins to warm up she starts worrying, even before she sees any. Then she becomes very afraid when she spots the first one and is reluctant to go outside, even in nice weather, because "There must be bugs out there somewhere." Although she has been afraid of bugs since she was a toddler, it seemed to be getting better for a while. Then, when she was five, the family went on a vacation and stayed at a seaside cabin for a week. Her parents expected to see a few bugs now and then, but what they didn't anticipate was a major outbreak of jumping bugs that covered the beach, took up residence in their towels, beach blankets, and clothes and seemed to haunt them wherever they went. This unfortunate experience solidified her bug fears. After what turned out not to be much of a vacation, she asked her parents to check her daily to make sure she didn't have any bugs, fleas, flies, tics or other creatures under her clothing when she came in from outside, even if she only went from the car to the house, and she pleaded with them to check her from head to toe before going to bed at night.

Now, occasionally, Sophia gets so involved in playing outside with her sister, she seems to forget about the bugs. But each time she begins to think about going outside, she becomes anxious and resistant. Given the choice, she would stay inside to play all day, every day. On the occasions when she does venture into the yard, she will shriek when a bug comes near her and run away without regard for safety. So her parents feel they have to be closely shadowing her once they leave the safety of their house, which places enormous restrictions on their lives.

The family is planning a camping trip at the beginning of the summer. They would also like to send Sophia to summer camp where her sister has gone for several years and raves about all the new kids she has met, the sports competitions, swimming, and many other outdoor activities. She would really like Sophia to go with her, and so would their parents, as Sophia would love it... if she weren't so afraid of bugs and thunderstorms. Understandably, they are very motivated to work on these fears intensely this winter and spring in an all-out effort to help her overcome them and have more opportunities to spend time with her sister, make new friends, and enjoy the great outdoors.

Finding the right therapist

Sophia's parents seek out and enlist the help of a therapist. The one they choose has done some work with children with developmental disabilities including autism, but he spends most of his time doing cognitive behavior therapy with anxious, typically developing children. This sounded like a reasonable background and a good match for their family, so they began working with Mr. Grant, a social worker, or Mike, as he liked to be called.

Step 1. Identify key trigger components of the feared object or situation: "Unbundle" the phobia

Mike works with the family to unbundle Sophia's thunderstorm fear. Her parents know she is scared of many environmental sounds, so the sound is probably a major contributing factor. But she loves music and especially playing it loud, *too* loud. She also likes hearing live music when her favorite groups come to town, which seems confusing and contradictory. Mike explains that more familiar and predictable sounds, like the music she plays over and over, are processed very differently than sudden, loud thunderclaps. However, he tells them that it is a positive sign that there are some sounds Sophia enjoys, as it may help in devising her treatment plan.

Thunder is nothing to clap about

Also, Mike explains, a sudden onset and deep rumbling sound, like thunder, tends to be associated with a greater anxiety response when the accompanying information they are picking up is also scary. This is why scary movies often feature music composed in minor keys played in certain patterns, and manipulating the tempo. This is done specifically to create an eerie, mysterious atmosphere. He also points out studies that have shown that the same music, played within a pleasant, cheerful or neutral context, does not make people feel scared. So if they can reduce Sophia's powerful and fearful associations with the sound of thunder, her fear may diminish. He digs up an article from *Time* magazine, about the natural fear response that certain tones evoke, and how the subject of the accompanying video or other visuals affects the listening experience (Haggin 2012), which the parents find very interesting.

Sophia is also startled by other things. Mike explains that her alarm goes off easily and triggers her fight–flight system. If the doorbell rings, for example, Sophia might give a quick yell and then calm when she realizes what it is. If her parents or sister approach her suddenly or from behind, she has the same response. Mike explains the surprise aspect of the thunder, in addition to its loudness, is probably activating her fight–flight response. Sophia is also afraid of the dark, and during daytime thunderstorms it tends to get dark as the storm clouds stack up, which is also a contributing factor.

They make a table of the likely components of her fear of thunderstorms.

FEAR: THUNDERSTORM

Volume of sound	Surprise aspect	Sudden darkness and rain

They go on to talk about her fear of bugs. Mike asks when it began and they fill him in on their terrible beach-bug vacation, but point out that the fear began long before that. He asks if she has ever been stung by any insect, which she has, but no more often than her sister and only by mosquitoes and maybe a few other harmless random bugs. She does get very upset when she gets stung, even by mosquitoes. Her sister was stung by a bee last summer and Sophia was far more upset than Carly was.

Mike makes a table of likely components related to her bug fears:

FEAR: BUGS

The flying around aspect	The feel on her skin	Fear of getting stung	Anticipating these fears

Step 2. Determine measures that reduce the child's anxiety

Self-regulating strategies

Sophia loves listening to music and is quite musical herself as are her parents. She especially likes rock music and blues from her parents' era so the family often listens to music together. Her parents always thought she had a natural sense of rhythm, so when she asked to take drum lessons, they were as enthusiastic as she was. Soon they noticed that playing the drums along with music was very soothing for her.

She also enjoys imitating the dancers on music videos, although she prefers doing her own original rhythmic routines, which she also finds soothing.

Co-regulating strategies

Although Sophia enjoys listening and performing solo, she enjoys it even more when her parents join in. She especially likes the frequent family "dance parties" in the living room. Although she is often serious, more so than her sister Carly and most children her age, Sophia's father has the magic touch and can get her laughing with a few activities they both enjoy, like fooling around with family photos on the iPad and distorting them. He taught her how to make funny mouths and noses and they compete to see who can make the silliest face. "Lookit Grandma!!" says Sophia, laughing hysterically as she makes her grandmother's face long and skinny and her ears big and pointy.

Step 3. Design levels of gradually increasing exposure to each component

Thunderstorms

Mike and Sophia's parents come up with a list of activities to include in the plan for desensitizing her to each terrifying aspect of thunderstorms. They craft a plan integrating Sophia's love of music and drumming into the process, which they believe will reduce her anxiety during the gradual exposures. The plan also incorporates her fear of fear; she will take back some control and pretend to "scare" the adults, which will help her co-regulate and remain calm while being exposed gradually to the sources of her fear.

Volume of sound	Surprise aspect	Sudden onset of darkness and rain
Play video of TS with S's favorite music in the background.	S controls start–stop of TS video and pretends to scare adults with sound.	Dim lights and play rain sounds.
Play video softly while playing S's favorite music in background.	Play TS video softly while you and S bang on drums when thunder cracks.	Turn lights on/off; play rain sound loudly with S in charge.
Play video, stopping before the sound is switched on and ask S how loud it should be.	Use a different TS video; you and S anticipate and play along on drum.	Turn lights off and create "Drum Thunder" with S.
Direct S to scare you, controlling the volume.	S surprises and scares you with sudden drum beat, increasing volume.	Play thunder video softly at night in dark room. Direct S to scare you.
	Direct S to surprise/ scare you with TS sound in video, gradually increasing volume.	Beat on drum outside at night and pretend it's thunder. S scares you.
		Bring tablet with video outside at night and play TS video. S controls stop-start and volume and scares you.

TS = Thunderstorm and S = Sophia

Beating back the bugs

Sophia's parents, with Mike's help, devise a plan, which includes the following activities: Sophia enjoys doing art projects so they incorporate pom-poms, which she especially likes, pretending they're bugs. They also buy some small plastic bugs and butterflies at a local party store. They begin with the activities in the first column, then proceed to the next column so Sophia can get used to things flying around and then feel small things touch her skin, which was key before adding a more emotionally-charged pretend routine around being stung.

The flying around aspect	The feel on her skin	Fear of getting stung	Anticipating these fears
Crumple up tiny pieces of tissue to create "tissue bugs" and toss them around at each other (if she thinks this if fun) or in the trash.	Make tissue bugs "land" on her/your arms and feet. Brush them off with exaggerated disgust/fear: "Eww! Get away!"	Go back to using tissue balls and pretend they are "stinging" you. Say, "Ouch! Get away," slapping them to the ground. Stomp on them. Throw them in the trash.	Pretend to be afraid throughout, first with tissue then with pom-poms, then with toy bugs, as they land on you.
Throw them so they pass by near the sides of her/your face/eyes as you play as long as she is still having fun.	Shift to using pom-poms.	Move on to pom-poms and plastic bugs when Sophia is ready.	Play on the front step outside. Go inside and come out saying, "There better not be bugs out here."

			Tell her to throw plastic bugs on to you. Tinker with the details until she thinks it's funny and repeat many times, swapping roles.
Advance to craft pom-poms playing as with the tissue.	Together glue on googly eyes and call them "bugs" as you play.	Use bug-related game apps like "Bugs and Buttons" so she can see and touch, moving, realistic bug images.	Bring toy bugs to the park/ beach and play these (now fun, presumably) games in anticipation of real bugs.
Add some googly eyes to these and call them bugs as you throw them around.	Make small plastic bugs "land" first on shoes, clothes, then on skin, brushing them away with playful exaggeration.	Distort bug images, as Sophia likes to do this with photos pretending the bugs sting you. "Squash," distort them.	
		Pretend the toy bugs sting you. Say "OUCH! You got me" and swipe them away. Scratching your skin as if it's itchy.	

Step 4. Proceed through the levels described in Step 2, combined with anxiety reducing strategies from Step 3

At first the gradual exposure plan they hatched around the thunderstorm didn't seem like it was going to work. The parents turned on the thunderstorm video Mike had given them, with the volume turned way down, which immediately sent Sophia scurrying from the room. They then turned it off and let her know the coast was clear. When she was comfortably settled and playing again, they turned it on, but with no sound at all this time and did not insist that she watch it. Having already set up her drum kit, she and her mother began singing as she drummed while the thunderstorm video ran silently on the computer nearby. Sophia, caught up in the music, became calm again, occasionally glancing at the video for a few seconds. Her father turned up the volume just a bit as Sophia happily drummed away. Once she got used to the video and audio playing simultaneously, they were able to proceed systematically through the rest of the activities.

Real thunder makes Sophia bolt

Early in the desensitization process there was one real thunderstorm which frightened Sophia. But a week later when another one occurred, she was more able to tolerate it. Rather than cowering in fear, she played her drums, trying to time her beats to accompany the thunder. Her preoccupation with cloudy skies and with the weather in general began to diminish; eventually she rarely asked about it. Not surprisingly, her parents were as pleased and relieved as she was, and were hoping that they had "sealed the deal" on this particular phobia.

Sophia loved the bug play, even more than the thunderstorm routine. She especially enjoyed stomping on the toy bugs and bombarding her father with them as soon as he came home from work. After a short time, less than a week of intensive bug play indoors, they ventured into the backyard, then to the park, and finally to the scene of the bug fiasco: the beach, while engaging in playful bug wars the whole time. As it was still early in the spring there were very few bugs to battle. But the ones they did encounter—the real ones—began to lose their power over her. As more bugs arrived along with the warmer weather Sophia's bug phobia continued to diminish. One day she proudly announced, "I don't even care if the mosquitoes bite me. I'll just shoo them away and squash them."

CHAPTER 6

TREATING WILL'S PHOBIA OF ENVIRONMENTAL SOUNDS, INCLUDING FLUSHING TOILETS, HAND DRYERS, AND VACUUM CLEANERS

Fear makes the wolf bigger than he is.
GERMAN PROVERB

All those booms and bangs and crashes scare me. I think something bad is going to happen and I want to run away and hide. WILL, AGE 7

Background

Will is a seven-year-old boy who is terrified of many common, everyday environmental sounds. His parents can't remember a time when he wasn't afraid of noises. They recall that as a baby, he often cried when they would use the vacuum cleaner or the garbage disposal, even operate the electric can opener. They generally worked around his sensitivities to sound by putting off doing chores that required the use of household gadgets when Will was around, or by choreographing an elaborate household ballet without the use of noisy machines. Sometimes one parent would take Will for a car ride while the other would spring into action and quickly vacuum the entire house, mow the lawn, and open a day's worth of canned cat food. But it was exhausting. As Will grew older he seemed to tolerate some sounds, like the less noisy kitchen appliances. But the vacuum cleaner continued to upset him, and he found bathroom sounds, especially the automatic flushing toilets and hand dryers in public restrooms, absolutely terrifying. When the family went on community outings, his parents were so preoccupied with finding a private "family bathroom" in a restaurant or shopping mall, that they hardly enjoyed themselves. They always carried tape to cover the sensor in case the toilet was one of those loud, automatic, electronically flushing ones, and they packed hand sanitizer and little towels so they could avoid hand dryers altogether. However, when there wasn't a private bathroom in the vicinity or when other people were using the facilities at the same time and Will could hear all those disturbing noises, he became paralyzed with fear and refused to go in, which often resulted in toileting accidents, abandoned plans, disappointments, and sometimes big arguments.

Becoming an expert in running interference

Will's parents continued to allay his fear of the vacuum cleaner by using it when he wasn't home or when he was sound asleep. On the rare occasions when they absolutely had to vacuum and he was there, he would race to his room and cover his ears. But the noise still made him nervous and upset. It was far more difficult to control circumstances at school, in the community or at the homes of friends and relatives. One day at an indoor gym, for example, another child spilled a box of crackers and the gym staff immediately brought out and turned on a small vacuum cleaner, right next to Will. He reacted intensely, screaming and crying. It was very likely a result of the noise, itself, but also a response to the disruption in his play and sudden onset of the scary noise; after all, what was a vacuum cleaner doing at the gym? Distressed about the actual event and now terrified about the possibility of a vacuum cleaner showing up unannounced, anywhere, Will refused to return to that indoor gym, a place where he had always felt comfortable and safe, a place he had always loved.

Scary school sounds

School was problematic for other reasons. The bathrooms were tolerable because there were no automatic flushers, just the old fashioned, hand-operated kind, and there were no hand dryers, just paper towels. But the announcements delivered via public address system through loudspeakers in every classroom caused him the same kind of distress. Will's school team agreed to let him use noise cancelling headphones, but they didn't cancel out all the noise, and his fear that "some noise might spill out" caused him a great deal of angst. As soon as he heard the first crackling sounds heralding the morning's announcements, he would shriek and run out of the classroom even when he had the headphones at his disposal.

Will did get special permission to go into the nurse's office during the scheduled morning announcements, as that was one place that was predictably quiet and speaker-free. But his anxiety escalated each morning, just before the regular announcements, as he worried about whether he would be able to get to the nurse's office in time. He also worried about whether there might be an unexpected announcement during the day, since that had happened on occasion—like the time the principal delivered a school-wide message mid-morning about a children's book author who was making a surprise visit to the school that afternoon.

Enlisting everyone's assistance

Discouraged and frustrated, Will's parents met with his school team to brainstorm some possible approaches and solutions. They all agreed to tackle the bathroom sound phobias first, because it was especially disruptive to family outings and caused Will to miss many recreational, sporting and social events that he would have otherwise enjoyed. His school team felt that any approach that would be successful with one phobia could be used to reduce his other related phobias during the school day. Before beginning, they wanted to begin working on his fear of the PA system as soon as they could and committed to keeping in close touch with his family, monitoring his progress and praising his efforts as well as his victories. While this was a big problem at school, his fear of public bathrooms was a big problem for the family, preventing them from going out to the mall, stores, restaurants or other community areas where he or the adult he was with might have to use a public bathroom. Hence the team decided to first work on the bathroom noises and then learn from that and move to working on the school loudspeaker issue.

Step 1. Identify key trigger components of the feared object or situation: "Unbundle" the phobia

Will's parents were certain his phobia was a result of both the unpredictability and sudden onset of the sounds of the toilet and hand dryer—the startle factor—as well as the noise itself. Beginning in infancy, Will had startled easily and would flinch and scream in response to any sudden change in the environment, in addition to the actual noise. The sound of the coffee grinder, a breaking glass, or a door or a window slamming in the wind had always frightened him. While they hoped his fears would dissipate over time, in fact they gradually expanded. True, he did become able to tolerate some sounds, like running water and his father's snoring. But he developed an intense fear of the possibility of one of the other dreaded sounds occurring. To Will, it felt like danger lurking around every corner.

Figure 6.1 summarizes how to unbundle this phobia.

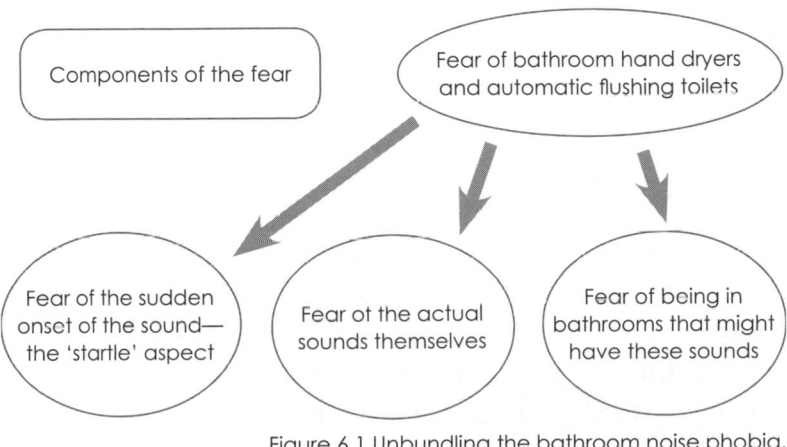

Figure 6.1 Unbundling the bathroom noise phobia.

Step 2. Determine measures that will reduce the child's anxiety

This step involves identifying strategies that will decrease the child's distress while increasing exposure. It is the step that is generally incorporated into CBT for typically developing children and is often quite successful in reducing their fearfulness. However, it is rarely attempted with children with ASD, particularly children with more severe or complex profiles, as it is difficult to decrease anxiety in a child who cannot independently or intentionally relax by using visualization, engage in guided breathing exercises and other demanding CBT techniques.

How to identify strategies that are likely to work

Specific strategies that work to decrease a child's anxiety vary from child to child and should be developed based on their interests and preferences as well as previous successes. Examples of self-regulating strategies (doing deep breathing, listening to favorite music, performing a designated job, such as taking pictures or recording data) will be discussed, as well as examples of co-regulating strategies (sharing slapstick humor with a favorite person; enjoying private jokes; singing together). How to develop new strategies will also be discussed.

Pinpointing special interests and strengths

Will greatly enjoyed time at home and especially playful, silly interactions with his family. His parents had often used humor when he was younger, to help him get through activities that were unpleasant or uncomfortable, such as buckling him into his car seat and getting him into and out of awkward, cumbersome winter clothing. Naturally, they sensed that incorporating humor into the process of gradual exposure was the right way to go, as it would make it less objectionable, and maybe even enjoyable—for Will and for them—while also decreasing his anxiety. Will also loved pretending with his stuffed animals and action figures, so it made sense to include some of his favorite toys in the process too. And he idolized and trusted his older brother, Mark, who was usually happy to do anything that would help Will. Mark was quite the performer and especially liked clowning around and making Will laugh. He felt sad when he saw how upset Will got about noises and how going to the bathroom was a major traumatic event when they went out. But he also felt frustrated and angry himself; his family stopped going to places he enjoyed, like the movies and miniature golf, because of Will's severe reactions. But in spite of the limitations that Will's struggles brought to family life, Mark knew how important his involvement was.

At his parents' request, Mark agreed to give Will a preview or demonstration of what was to come, either by actually doing a task that was likely to cause him anxiety, role playing, or acting it out with toys. The idea was that Will would see that there was no mystery or threat involved; that it was no big deal; and that he would know exactly what to expect and what it would sound like. If Mark could do it, so could he! So Mark happily went through the motions of getting a haircut (even when he didn't need one), got the flu shot first, and demonstrated over and over how to put on and take off his snow boots. He constantly added activities to his repertoire, making a major contribution to his family's well-being.

Favorite toys add to the fun

Like many children his age, Will loved electronic games, and Angry Birds was the "app of the moment." He loved the characters so much that he got several stuffed birds as presents and took them on family outings and to bed, always. So including the birds into the gradual exposure process would surely entice and motivate Will.

Step 3. Design levels of gradually increasing exposure to each component

Will's parents now had a basic plan. They would integrate his favorite toys, people, and pastimes into the activities they planned, first in the safety and security of their home and in a more distant and representational way, using video—and then out in the community, in the actual environments that had caused him anxiety. This gradual step-by-step approach would increase exposure and very likely result in low levels of discomfort, but at the same time, Will would be engaging enjoyable and highly engaging activities, which would likely reduce his anxiety to some degree.

Using the ubiquitous YouTube

Will's parents decided to produce their own film, which is now easier and faster than one can imagine. They discovered that virtually any type of sound and sound effect is available on YouTube, so they downloaded some video clips of different automatic flush toilets and hand dryers. They also shot some of their own videos using their phone cameras, in the bathrooms in venues they often visited, including the mall, an indoor playspace, a couple of restaurants, and a bookstore—when they were empty and with permission from security or on-site managers, of course. In addition to the sound effects and in order to incorporate both interactive humor and his beloved older brother and their natural clowning around play, Will's parents made several silly video clips starring Mark, activating a noisy flush toilet and a hand dryer in a public bathroom. Mark was quite the comedian anyway and loved playing with Will, performing for him and especially making him laugh—anything that would help so that they could go on more family outings.

This became quite the family production and everyone pitched in. With a little parental coaching and direction, Mark made a series of videos with his phone camera, targeting each of the components within the fear bundle:

1. First Mark pretended, with great anticipation and exaggerated effect that he was going to push the hand dryer button. But instead, he "missed" his mark, fell over in a slapstick manner and laughed. The reasoning was that by watching this brief routine, Will would be exposed to a very basic level of practice in anticipating the sound of the hand dryer—but without actually having to tolerate any sound at all. And he would be doing so while laughing with and at Mark.

2. For the next level of exposure, their parents suggested that Mark put on a big, dramatic display of slowly counting to three and then pressing the button and immediately covering his ears with his hands while smiling. This would communicate to Will that Mark wasn't truly distressed and give him more practice tolerating the sudden onset of the noise—the startle aspect—but in a familiar, controlled, and humorous way with his favorite person. Here the reasoning is that by watching Mark's counting and moving towards the dryer, Will would

learn to prepare for and then hear the noise. By covering his ears while smiling, Mark humorously conveys empathy and reassurance, while increasing exposure to the feared noise.

3. The next level of exposure included a clip of Mark activating the hand dryer with prior warning, just as he did previously. But this time, he added exaggerated, cartoonish anger. He shook his finger at the offending device, and scolded it, saying, "NO NO! TOO LOUD!" until the dryer stopped. Mark added an unscripted, "Why thank you, hand dryer," in a silly voice and blew it a kiss, something he knew Will would find uproariously funny. Then the family film crew made a similar set of clips around the automatic toilet flusher, incorporating approaching it slowly, activating the switch and laughing and repeatedly reprimanded the terrible toilet. How could a seven-year-old boy not find this funny?

The characters from Will's current favorite iPad game, Angry Birds, opened up even more possibilities. Mark played puppet master and put Will's big stuffed Red Bird in some silly and compromising situations in a similar set of videos. Since they often engaged in rough and tumble play with the Bird this was familiar and fun territory for Will. In one video clip, Mark made the bird flush the toilet, hiccup, burp, and say, "Excuse me" in a loud, annoying voice. Then he accidentally dropped the Bird in the sink, setting off the automatic faucet, splashing water everywhere and creating chaos.

The goal of these video clips was to create scenes that Will would be motivated to watch because they were likely to be funny to him, involving his brother clowning around as well as involving Angry Birds, which he enjoyed a great deal. The video clips also included some of the sounds that Will was afraid of.

There are two components of video that lend themselves to the gradual exposure process: First, the volume can be initially turned way down, or off, gradually increasing it as the child is able to tolerate it. Hence the child is able to experience first a small amount of the actual sound, then increasing amounts.

A second advantage of using video clips is that repeated watching removes the startle/surprise element of the onset of the sound. Children generally like to watch favorite clips over and over. After Will has watched it a few times, he will know and be able to anticipate exactly when the sound part will begin, allowing him to increasingly tolerate the sound aspect of the phobia, without having to at the same time tolerate the surprise aspect.

Eventually once he knows he can readily tolerate the sound, the surprise aspect will not be as distressing, as the sound itself will be less distressing. However, sometimes fear of the surprise aspect persists and then can be worked on separately, through video and real life.

By the end of that day, they had far more footage than they needed and began to organize and sequence it. They were ready to tackle the problem with the expectation that Will would slowly and comfortably experience the sounds he feared in a new way, experiencing less and less anxiety with each exposure.

Step 4. Proceed through the levels described in Step 2, including the anxiety reducing strategies from Step 3

The parents were now ready to begin the gradual exposure process. They transferred the video clips to the computer and played them repeatedly so Will could become increasingly familiar and comfortable with his own anticipation, with the sudden onset of the sounds, and with the sounds themselves. They postulated that as Will's anxiety began to diminish, they would go to the actual bathrooms at some of the locales they frequented, the mall being the obvious first choice, and monitor his level of anxiety there. If Will's anxiety has dissipated sufficiently, they would begin to work on another component of fear bundle. If he continued to experience a high level of fear, they would take a step back, repeat the process several times, altering aspects, such as the speed at which they introduced the sequence, changing the order of events, or increasing or reducing the humor element.

First Will's parents showed him the video clip of Mark pretending to activate the hand dryer, missing and then collapsing in a fit of laughter. Initially Will turned and backed away, looking in the other direction. But when he heard Mark's laughter he smiled, peeked at it, watched more closely and then said, "Again!" He watched the video several times, with increasing interest and enthusiasm each time.

Their parents then told Will—and demonstrated—that they were turning the sound off. They offered to show Will the next few video clips, and he was equally enthusiastic, laughing continuously as he watched his brother and the big Red Bird clowning around with the hand dryer and flusher, the very objects that had caused him so much fear and angst. His parents turned up the volume slightly, to begin desensitizing him to the sound. But Will, very experienced and skilled in using all kinds of electronics, noticed the sound icon appear on the screen, and threw the phone, clearly anxious and anticipating louder, scarier noises.

Aspiring actor antics

To further tackle the problem, Will's father, who loved imitating actors and accents, mannerisms and noises went back to the drawing board. He made an even sillier version of the hand dryer and toilet sounds. Will's intense fear response began to diminish, as he watched the videos over and over. He laughed as his father added funny faces and exaggerated mannerisms to the routine, like dramatically clapping his hands over his mouth, when Will yelled, "Stop." When he told his father, "Go," he resumed the silly noises and faces, giving him complete control.

While all this was going on, Will's mother surreptitiously and gradually turned the sound up on the original video. Will didn't seem distressed; he was too involved in playing the stop and go sound game with his father. If Will had become upset she would have turned the volume off again and they would have taken a step back and paired the sound with familiar audio from Angry Birds, possibly, which might have been more palatable and calming for Will.

Totally enthralled by the videos starring his brother and his Angry Bird, Will asked to watch the original videos again, with the sound on very low. He burst out in laughter every time he heard the bird burp, thanks to Mark's sound effects, and he loved the silly jokes that were scattered throughout. In fact, it was difficult to get him to stop watching!

Mark and Will's parents decided to step things up and seize what appeared to be a developing momentum. In an effort to continue the desensitization process they planned a trip to the mall, where they would orchestrate a similar scenario, in a real bathroom. But things didn't go as smoothly, at least at first. Will's anxiety began to escalate as they approached the bathroom, and he had a full-blown tantrum when his father tried to get him inside. So they retreated and they went to the ice cream shop to rethink their plan.

They decided to make a video of Mark and the Angry Bird in the mall bathroom, showing him walking through the mall, and making Angry Bird be a little scared to go in the bathroom. Once in the bathroom, they would repeat scenes from the previous videos. Will liked watching all of them.

The family made another mall trip, bringing along Mark and the Angry Bird. This time they wouldn't force Will to go into the bathroom but rather, they would play together near the bathroom. Will was quite comfortable this time. He even ventured in to the bathroom for a quick look around, to see where they made the video. His mother seized on this moment and made a quick video of Will inside the bathroom, to show later as a reminder to Will that he was very calm and actually happy.

They also thought the surprise element of the sounds could still be scaring Will. So they isolated and targeted this factor, by finding comparable sounds on their phone, using the website, Soundsnap. They played a variety of games with these sounds, turning the volume way down low, then gradually louder and louder and they made up and sang silly songs, peppering them with the offending sound, e.g. They sang "Old Macdonald had a FLUSHING-SOUND" His parents varied the length and volume, inserting and synchronizing their custom "soundtrack" as a surprise element, with Angry Bird playing. Any activity with an anticipatory element lends itself to practicing the experience of surprise, which often leads to a happy, shared experience, even if it didn't start out that way. A Jack-in-the-Box is a prime example.

Bathrooms in new places continue to cause Will some discomfort, although he is usually able to use them when he has to. Now that his family has a good sense of how this process works and how Will has been largely successful working through it, they share their experience with his school team. They, too, begin to craft a plan for desensitizing him to the announcements.

Summary

Will had a longstanding heightened sound sensitivity that had resulted in several sound-related phobias that were interfering with his home and school life. For a long time school and family had worked to help Will avoid these situations. However, unbundling his phobia around automatic toilet flushing and hand dryers, helping him increasingly tolerate the sounds, then the surprise element of the sound, using home-made video with a great deal of personalized humor incorporated into this, helped Will overcome these fears. This process was pleasurable for Will throughout. The family never pushed him to tolerate more than he was comfortable with. While it involved a lot of time on the family's part, the time put in was fun as well, much more fun than having Will scared and upset. And the result, that they could go places with Will using public bathrooms without distress, reflected a real improvement in their family life. They were ready to tackle Will's other fears with optimism and confidence.

CHAPTER 7

TREATING MICHAEL'S PHOBIA OF INJECTIONS AND BLOOD DRAWS

Our anxiety does not come from thinking about the future, but from wanting to control it.
KHALIL GIBRAN

Background

Michael is a sweet five-year-old boy with ASD who is nonverbal and communicates primarily through behavioral means. His family and preschool team know if he is happy or upset about something, and they usually know what he wants or what is distressing to him. His favorite activity is finding beloved Elmo, Thomas the Tank Engine, and The Wiggles videos on YouTube and watching them alone on his iPad. He also enjoys running around outside. He is most socially connected with his parents during bathtime, or roughhousing in the living room, building forts with the sofa cushions, and sometimes blowing up balloons and letting them fly around the room.

Michael doesn't like things being done *to* him. He often resists dressing, teethbrushing, and having his hair washed and combed, but his parents have found he is more tolerant when they slow down the process and enlist his help, like getting him to pull his shirt down, put toothpaste on the toothbrush and put the shampoo in his hair.

Injections instill fear

While he may get annoyed occasionally, his upsets are usually not severe, with one exception: he becomes extremely distressed when he has to have a vaccination, booster shot or any injection or when he has his blood drawn. Because of a medical condition, he has to have his blood drawn monthly in addition to the usual childhood shots. This has been a significant source of distress for him and as well as for his parents and medical providers. He starts screaming and tries to get away when they approach the lab where he has blood drawn. By the time he arrives in the waiting room, he is exhausted, drenched in tears and still crying, with his frazzled parents doing everything they can to comfort him. An extra technician has to assist during the actual blood draw, and Michael sits on his mother's lap squirming and screaming throughout the process. Once it is over, he starts to calm down and generally falls asleep soon after, very likely from exhaustion.

Ironically, his parents noticed, he always seemed to have a high tolerance for pain and rarely cried, even as a baby, when he fell and cut his knee or bumped his head. They thought, understandably, that the actual pain of the needle prick might not affect him at all, although it was difficult to really understand his pain experience, as he didn't yet have a way to accurately describe it or communicate his feelings.

Michael's parents had tried showing him his favorite videos in the car on the way to and at the lab, to distract and entertain him, as this sometimes got him through long car trips, grocery shopping, and other activities he didn't especially enjoy. At the lab, however, and even on the car trip there, he was too upset to focus and pushed his iPad away—he even tried to throw it on the floor while kicking and screaming. His enjoyment of the videos couldn't compete with his distress about having his blood drawn. His parents felt he may have been angry or offended at even being offered the iPad, as if they just didn't understand what he was trying to tell them, namely, that he did not want to go to the lab, was terrified to be there, and had no control over it.

Not ready for social stories

Equally concerned over his distress, Michael's school staff had made a social story with photographs of all the steps involved in getting a shot or blood draw. They read it to him several times, as they found this often helped preschoolers get through new or challenging experiences. However, Michael had not shown much interest in the stories. Maybe they were too abstract, too distant from his actual experience given his developmental level, and he could not process and then use the information or illustrations to help him make sense of his actual experience.

Step 1. Identify key trigger components of the feared object or situation: "Unbundle" the phobia

Since Michael didn't like people dressing or bathing him, his parents realized that having blood drawn would fall into the same category—or a worse one—since it also involved being confined, having his arm restrained, sitting still for what seemed like forever, and then feeling pain. They also could see that his fears had spread to all things related to having his blood drawn, from pulling up to the building in the car, to going in the waiting room, and probably to many other, visual, tactile, and olfactory components related to the whole experience. He clearly showed anticipatory fear. While

Michael's parents felt, realistically, that he might continue to be uncomfortable just before and during blood draws, they were hoping to reduce the intensity of his fear overall, and possibly even eliminate his distress beforehand.

They couldn't be sure of all the components contributing to Michael's phobia, or what they might discover as they moved through the gradual exposure process, but they identified the following as elements to work on initially, in isolation and together:

1. Being confined on a parent's lap in a big chair with his arm stabilized or restrained.

2. Being exposed to medical materials, such as the tourniquet, alcohol wipes, tubing, syringe, and band aids.

3. The locations involved (parking lot, inside of the lab building, waiting room, blood draw room).

4. The uniformed lab technicians.

5. Fear of fear, the element preceding and propelling the whole experience.

6. The pain of the needle as it punctured his skin, although they were not entirely sure this was a factor.

Step 2. Determine measures that reduce the child's anxiety: Self-regulating strategies

Warm-up before work

Michael's parents and school team noticed that he was generally composed and more focused on tasks after he had been running around outside or in a good roughhousing play session. They decided to engage in high-energy activities as a warm-up exercise before trying to work on the gradual exposure processes, many of which would involve sitting still.

Although Michael calmly and happily watched his favorite shows on the iPad, it was difficult to engage him during that time— or even to get his attention at all, so they decided to not use these those videos initially. However, they did consider incorporating them once his fear subsided at least a little, especially before and during the blood draw. Watching videos might further distract and calm him then.

Co-regulating strategies

At home Michael enjoyed roughhousing on the sofa, with his parents. At school he was most enthusiastic in sessions with his OT, maybe because she incorporated a lot of movement activities like swinging. Sometimes his OT and speech therapist did a co-treatment session, during which he was happy, calm, and more interactive than usual; his ability to focus and use his few signs and communicative gestures clearly increased.

While Michael wasn't yet doing pretend play, he often carried around a big blue stuffed train, reminiscent of his beloved Thomas the Tank Engine. He liked to sleep with it too.

Step 3. Design levels of gradually increasing exposure to each component

Michael's parents considered each of the elements they had unbundled, identified the activities that were calming and enjoyable for him, and came up with the following working plan:

Sitting confined on a parent's lap in a big chair with his arm outstretched and stabilized

The family had an old deteriorating recliner chair with big stuffed arms that they had inherited from Michael's grandfather. Nobody actually sat in it; it was generally used as a place to put coats and jackets, laundry, and mail to sort through. It would also make a great blood draw practice chair. So Michael's parents cleared it off and put some of his stuffed animals in it, to make it more appealing.

They planned to first turn it into a fun spot, a place where he would want to play and relax, before turning it into a lab chair. They would then gradually add single components of the blood draw experience, monitoring Michael's reactions. He loved having his arms stroked and tickled, so they would add that to the chair experience. Sometimes he would even hold his arm out and say, "t-t-t!" his way of asking for "tickles." They considered gradually adding material to wrap around his arm, just as the lab tech did during a blood draw.

The medical materials: tourniquet, alcohol wipes, tubing, wrap, bandaid

Michael's parents enlisted the help of the lab and asked for a small supply of whatever tools and materials they could spare in order to simulate the lab experience. Everything but the syringes and needles was made available to them.

They also asked to borrow some lab coats. This was against lab policy; however, the school nurse had a few leftover from her job at a hospital and was only too happy to loan them out.

Michael's parents would first casually put the materials out, hoping they would capture his interest. If Michael didn't notice or spontaneously play with them, they would include them (somehow!) while roughhousing. Even if Michael rejected or removed them, it would increase his exposure. Maybe they could hide a few tourniquets in the sofa cushions and turn their play session into a game: who could find the most on the floor as they played. If so they would try this with their other medical props as a precursor to more direct play with them.

Michael's OT would also join the case and set up similar scenarios during his therapy session at school. As he was used to finding hidden objects in the bean table or encased in Theraputty, she could do the same with bandaids or packaged alcohol wipes.

Combining exposure to several unbundled elements once Michael had become comfortable with each separately
Once Michael became comfortable with the recliner and medical materials, his parents planned to combine the two, gradually increasing exposure by re-enacting the blood draw experience, while also including the tickle game, to add a calming element.

The locations: parking lot, inside of the lab building, waiting room, blood draw room
It could be that once Michael was no longer afraid about blood draws, his fears about the associated environments would dissipate. However, simply being in those familiar settings could create distress regardless, as they had become a trigger and evoked such negative experiences. Michael's parents decided to do many "drive by's" during which they simply would visit the lab, maybe to get something from the vending machine in the lobby, rather than have blood drawn. They wanted to draw on Michael's interest in watching videos on his iPad in the process. But would he understand he was just going to go to the lab without having blood drawn? That had never happened. They tried driving into the parking lot on only one occasion, but he became very distressed.

They decided to back up and add some preliminary video steps. First they made a couple of videos of driving into the parking lot, with the Elmo song as an accompaniment and a stuffed Elmo jumping out of Michael's car seat. Then they carried Elmo into the building, down the hall, all the way to the waiting room, while voicing Elmo, saying, "No! No!" but in a playful way, with Elmo quickly regaining his (silly) composure. They then made a few more waiting room videos starring Elmo in some familiar positions, such as seated in the lab chair, having his blood drawn and objecting, but then tolerating the procedure.

The lab staff in their uniforms

Michael's parents dressed up in oversized white shirts and paper towel masks, which amused Michael to no end. They also found dozens of videos on the Internet of hospital staff in lab coats, draped in medical gowns, donning various head coverings and masks, which Michael found very intriguing and not frightening.

Fear of fear, the feelings experienced prior to anything actually happening

Michael's parents infused the videos with fear of fear by voicing Elmo's objections loud and clear when he had his blood drawn. His mother joined the cast, too, also pretending to object to having her blood drawn. The plan was to include the seriously funny videos into their play routines on the recliner once Michael had become somewhat desensitized to the actual medical props.

Michael's mother coincidentally had to have some blood drawn during a routine check-up, so she made a funny video with her phone camera, pretending to be a little afraid and then going through with it, and they quickly uploaded this sequence to Michael's iPad.

Possibly the pain of the needle piercing his skin

Michael's parents consulted with his OT about the pain issue. She wasn't certain and suggested they experiment with different textures and sensations on his arm. For example, they presented and then gauged his response to playing with and then being touched by warm (but not hot) objects, coarse and itchy fabrics, and then frozen teething toys. He especially enjoyed the cold feeling on his skin. They found a set of freezable trains and carefully integrated them into his play routines.

Step 4. Proceed through the levels described in Step 2, combined with anxiety reducing strategies from Step 3

With this plan in place Michael's parents and OT tackled each step. They were immediately successful with some of the activities, but Michael objected to or wasn't interested in others. So they revisited and revised some of their initial ideas.

He especially enjoyed playing in the big, overstuffed, deteriorating but newly available recliner. His parents padded it with even more cushions and he loved roughhousing with them in it. When they added tickling, he willingly extended his arm, a first step toward appropriate positioning for a blood draw.

He also enjoyed rifling through the cushions in search of hidden tourniquets, gauze, and bandaids, then throwing them around the room and onto the floor. For some reason, this activity truly tickled his funnybone, allowing his parents to increase exposures to the medical props he encountered at the lab. They stepped it up a notch and began tickling his arm with the tourniquet. Eventually, while he was in the big old chair, they gradually added additional materials from the lab, including the alcohol wipes and rubber tubing.

In order to entice him with the home-made videos, the ones he refused to watch on his iPad previously, Michael's teacher arranged to project them on the classroom Smartboard. He happily included the videos in a unit on health and thought that Michael's classmates would benefit too, since they also had to get routine shots and blood draws. Some of them even went to the same clinic. At school Michael was far more interested, even excited to see his parents on the big screen. He scurried up to the front of the room to get a closer look, laughing and, it seemed, jumping for joy. Michael's classmates also enjoyed Elmo's amusing adventures at the lab and recognized Michael's parents too, very impressed that they were co-starring with their fuzzy red hero. Although not part of the preschool curriculum, this was time well-spent, as most children (and many adults!) find it somewhat unpleasant at best to get shots and have blood drawn.

Incorporating the child's objections—putting them in charge of the degree of exposure

When they began incorporating more realistic procedures into their play routines, such as placing the tourniquet or rubber tubing around Michael's arm, he initially began to get upset and pushed them away. His mother, in an attempt to express what she believed he was thinking, yelled at the tourniquet, saying, "No, No! Go AWAY!" and then hid it behind her back. She then snuck it back onto the chair although not onto his arm again yet. They played the "No no, Go away" game several times over. Michael joined in, requesting that she continue, as it was starting to be fun.

She increased the exposure and moved on to actually putting the tourniquet on, but not around his arm. When he objected she threw it to the floor in a cartoonish way, yelling, "No, no, no!" Michael seemed to lose interest and settled down into the cozy chair with Elmo. His mother speculated that he may have become more comfortable; as she proceeded to wrap it around his arm loosely, he barely noticed. He did seem tired, so she got his iPad and he watched videos as she continued to gently affix his wrapped arm to the arm rest.

Once Michael had watched the original videos at school a few times with his classmates, he also expressed an interest in watching them at home on his iPad. He did this over and over, and memorizing the funny parts and anitcipating them with delight, as he did with his favorite Thomas videos.

Michael's parents felt he was now ready for a trip to the lab parking lot, and maybe a short visit to the waiting room without even a hint of having his blood drawn. They brought along Elmo and posted the videos on the iPad so that Michael could watch them as they drove in and out of the parking lot several times, eventually parking the car and turning off the engine. They re-enacted Elmo's objection to the parking lot and having a full-blown tantrum, which Michael thought was hilarious. He continued to be happy and relaxed until they got to the front door. That was a little too close for comfort. So they sat on the steps and played and waited until he calmed down; they didn't want to leave when he was upset, as he might have been confused.

Was he really going to have his blood drawn? Did his parents change their minds? If so, why? Would he have to come back tomorrow? They went home, having decided to push the envelope a little further next time.

After a few more blood-free, shot-free visits, Michael was beginning to make some real progress. Each time he got a little further, first inside the front door, then a walk down the corridor, then into the waiting room and eventually, peeking into the blood draw room, and finally sitting in the chair.

He and his parents continued to play through the scenario at home and he watched the videos several more times at school. Soon he was able to make trips to the lab with little or no fears, including sitting down in the real chair and rolling up his sleeve.

Finally, about two months after embarking on this journey, Michael was able to engage in every step of the process. And he did the unimaginable: he had his blood drawn, only crying when the needle pierced his skin but not panicking, and then recovering quickly. His mother captured this crowning achievement on her phone camera, which, not surprisingly, he wanted to watch over and over and over.

Summary

At first glance, Michael did not appear to be the ideal candidate for this process. He was quite young, almost completely nonverbal, and enjoyed only a few activities. Moreover, he did most of them solo. When Michael's parents and school staff first began this program, they admitted they were not terribly optimistic. They certainly didn't think his phobias would diminish to the extent they did. But with slow, thoughtful exposures to the individual components contributing to his fear responses and tackling them one by one, and pairing the objects and events with more fun and enjoyable activities and events, his treatment team was able to create new emotional memories, strengthen their bond with him through shared activities and help him at least tolerate some of the medical procedures that would likely be necessary throughout his life.

CHAPTER 8

TREATING JACOB'S PHOBIA OF LOSING GAMES AND NOT BEING FIRST

I don't *want* to be first. I *have* to be first. I really, really can't wait. Maybe other kids can but I can't. My body needs to go first.

JACOB, AGE 8

Background

Jacob is a bright, energetic eight-year-old who was diagnosed with Asperger syndrome when he was four. He has always attended inclusive public schools, with a great deal of support during his first few years and more recently, with only organizational help and support around problem solving with classmates and occasionally for clarification on academic assignments. He meets with the school psychologist "when needed," as stipulated in his Individualized Education Plan (IEP), usually to work on an immediate problem, and with a private therapist every other week outside of school. He has a lot of interests, including geography and the weather, and he also likes to play board and video games. He is beginning to take an interest in sports, especially baseball. Although he just began to play on a school team last season, he knows all the rules and every team's standing in the major leagues, which impresses his teammates. He has a great deal of difficulty participating as a member of a team and taking directions from his coach and teammates; there is a great deal of language and nuanced communication between players and coaches that he often can't follow and misinterprets. He doesn't always "get" what is happening around him, or what is expected of him, or why. And, he often feels like the coach or his teammates are "barking orders" at him and that upsets him.

For 3rd grader, 2nd base is 1st choice

One of the biggest problems is that Jacob always wants to be first in the line-up and he wants to play second base. *Only* second base. He is a reasonably good player, although he hasn't been playing for years and years like many of his teammates. But everyone on the team wants to include him and see him succeed. They have known Jacob since kindergarten and are used to his quirkiness and they truly like him. The first season he played, they let him go first and excused the fact that he could be a "spoiled sport." But now in 3rd grade they are not as tolerant and are finding his rigidity and tendency to get angry, scream, and stomp off the field very disruptive, upsetting—and kind of embarrassing.

Jacob has also become more and more intolerant of losing games. He used to sulk a little, but recovered fast. Now, when his team loses, he bursts into tears and runs off the field yelling, "It's not fair! We should have won!" Or he goes on and on about a bad call that the umpire made. When his team loses, he refuses to shake hands with the other team after the game or talk to his own teammates, sometimes for days.

Despite many discussions with his coach, parents, and school staff, Jacob's behaviors show no sign of diminishing. Parents and his coach tried a reward system for "being a good sport," talking to him and listing what that involved and while he quickly memorized the list that didn't help him in the moment. He even says, "I know it's my fault. I am going to try harder. But I just can't stand it. I need to be first. It feels wrong when I'm not first."

Good coaching means more than winning

Jacob's coach has been working with him for the past few weeks in anticipation of the spring season, which is about four months away. He is committed to Jacob's successful participation, but he has an obligation to all his other players too. While he realizes that Jacob has some special needs and that his brain works a little differently, he doesn't want to play favorites, nor does he want to "feed the flame," and continue to cater to Jacob's whims or fears. This, he feels, would alienate his teammates and could lead to scapegoating and isolation for Jacob. For example, if the team loses—and chances are they will, at some point during the season—his teammates might blame it on a poor line-up strategy and point the finger at Jacob. ("If someone else were the lead-off batter, we woulda won…")

The coach has consulted with Jacob's parents, the school psychologist, and his outside therapist in an effort to address the problem positively and in a way that will not single him out, i.e. as the only player who gets special privileges and is handled with kid gloves. Jacob's therapist, Ms. West, who has met with him regularly for more than a year, wants to help too. She has proposed that they try using a four-step model in order to identify the possible cause(s) of and reduce his rigidity about being first at bat, and his extreme emotional reaction to not winning. They are all related, she believes, and even if there is no quick fix for everything, she is optimistic that the intensity of his reactions may diminish. While they have touched upon these problems in the past, they have never gotten past the talking phase, with Ms. West making some casual suggestions and Jacob saying he would try them but not entirely understanding exactly what to do. This time, she proposes a more systematic approach based on his unique profile and especially on his preferences. She has taken several courses in CBT and this approach draws heavily from it. And she has had some success in treating both adults and children for a variety of behaviors that interfere with their daily functioning and success, including rigid thinking and phobias.

Since baseball season was a few months away, this was the ideal time to target some of Jacob's difficulties in a safe, non-pressured setting, when the stakes weren't high. He would have numerous opportunities to practice new, more positive and less anxiety-provoking ways of experiencing losing and striking out, then translate those new feelings onto the field during the actual season.

Step 1. Identify key trigger components of the feared object or situation: "Unbundle" the phobia

At their first meeting, Jacob and Ms. West begin talking about what happens on the field when he arrives for a game. Jacob wanted to fix those problems too and was able to be very specific about his experiences: "I feel fine in the locker room at first and I like putting on my uniform with my friends, and I'm glad that my parents are sitting in the bleachers waiting for me. Everybody is excited and happy and talking about the game. I try to join in the conversation, but then I get all nervous and I don't know what to say. And I have to hurry up and get ready and I'm always the last one to get all my stuff on, and I get all tangled up." He continued: "Then we go to the dugout and the coach starts talking about the game and what he knows about the other team, who's a good hitter, how the pitcher throws and stuff like that. That's when I start feeling upset. I *have* to be first at bat. I don't want to just sit around and wait to get up 4th or 5th—or never. I've tried all the other things you talked about, like taking deep breaths and bringing a fidget toy, but it doesn't help." Very aware of his feelings, he went on and on: "I just sit there and I want to scream. If I have to wait, I get really upset and think, 'what if I strike out?' If I go first I won't strike out but if I don't, well I think I will. And then if I do strike out that makes me more upset. Everyone on the team probably blames me. And then if we lose I really hate it. It makes me so sad and angry, like I could have done something to make us win. And everyone else is blaming me for losing."

After an extensive interview with Jacob, his parents and the coach, Ms. West asks Jacob if she can attend his next game, and he agrees. Based on Jacob's own report and her observation, they figure out that there are several triggers that feed his anxiety.

Jacob had always gotten overwhelmed easily. He could see "the big picture" but had trouble breaking it down into small, doable steps and tackling one at a time. He also had trouble deciphering complicated and multi-step verbal directions and missed a lot of details. So the busy, crowded locker room was likely contributing to his anxiety. While he was trying to find matching socks and lace up his cleats, there was noise and laughter, too much action, and too many different conversations going on.

In the past, Jacob's parents had seen his discomfort increase when he had too much to do. He was not a multitasker! When he came home from school, he immediately wanted to play outside, visit his friend Bill, and play video games. But he knew he had homework in three different subjects, had to watch his favorite TV program, take a bath, and read stories with his Dad before bed. He couldn't imagine getting it all done and felt defeated before taking the first step. Inevitably he would become angry, dig in his heals and insist on doing things his way.

Unbundling the phobia

Jacob's parents and therapist hypothesized that there were some components in the situation that raised Jacob's baseline anxiety, causing him to be more easily distressed. Specifically, they unbundled *his baseline higher anxiety* into these two components:

1. High activity/chaos in the locker room—not understanding, not knowing what to say.

2. Having to sit and listen as the coach talks about the game.

They speculated that if he could start playing the game with a lower baseline anxiety, he would have more tolerance in general for the specific trigger issues, such as not being able to play second base or being on the losing team, once they worked on these issues.

They decided to make a short-term plan to address these issues: For the first weeks of practice and the first few games until Jacob could better tolerate not being first and maybe losing, they all, including Jacob, agreed that he would arrive with his uniform on and ready to play. His parents would drop him off at the field so he could skip the locker room. This would be the basic plan for now, and once the rest of practice was going more smoothly, they would add the locker room component back in, gradually and step-by-step.

Having to sit and listen as the coach talked about the game was a time when Jacob's anxiety began to mount. It was really challenging for him to focus; he did not understand much of what the coach was talking about. While his treatment team considered having him also skip this part at first, they felt it would be more confusing and anxiety-provoking for Jacob to begin practice late. They asked the coach if he would be open to accompanying his discussion and pep talk with simple illustrations, which often helped Jacob at school, since he was not able to follow fast-paced, lecture-style teaching. The coach, a "computer guy" in his work life, was very interested in this suggestion. He quickly developed schematic, a clear graphic chart that visually presented what he wanted each team member to be doing in various positions, and he began e-mailing these to the players before every practice.

All the players and several of the parents were very pleased with this new addition to practice, and it was of great help to Jacob, who could now understand the strategies and prepare in advance for practice. He gained a much better understanding of the game—and much more confidence.

Components of the fear: Needing to be first at bat

1. Believing if he is not first, he is likely to strike out.

2. Fear of striking out; believing if he strikes out, he alone will be blamed; everybody will be mangy; and everything will be horrible.

3. The surprise element of striking out—that he didn't know in advance if he would strike out or not. Nobody does!

Components of the fear: Losing the game

1. Feeling that losing the game is horrible and unfair.

2. Feeling that losing means his teammates would blame him and be mean to him.

3. Anticipating that the team might lose. When the other team was up by more than one run Jacob would begin to feel anxious, irritable, and preoccupied with the thought of losing.

4. The surprise element of losing: he didn't know in advance if the team would win or lose.

Step 2. Determine measures that will reduce the child's anxiety

In addition to playing baseball, Jacob, an only child, liked being around a few friends, his dog, and his neighbor Bill, an older man who lived alone and always had time for Jacob. Bill told him stories about "the old days," often embellishing them with dramatic tales of voyages to exotic lands or impending disasters that were averted.

Even if there seemed to be no hope or a way to escape, Bill's stories always ended happily, and Jacob liked that.

He especially liked fantasy stories about animals with amazing powers and real people, mostly sports figures, and also superheroes who combated evil and saved the world. So enlisting Bill's assistance and using the characters from his stories might help Jacob cope with his own potential disasters as well.

Jacob also liked watching cartoons, especially Disney characters.

When Jacob got overwhelmed, he would sometimes feel better if he took a break, listened to a few of his favorite Disney CDs or watched a couple of cartoons. Mickey Mouse and Goofy often provided some much-needed comic relief, distraction, and the fuel he needed to go back to his work.

Step 3. Design levels of gradually increasing exposure to and tolerance of each component: Decreasing stress while increasing exposure

Needing to be first at bat—fear of striking out
STRIKING OUT ON PURPOSE IN "BALLOON BASEBALL" PLAY

Jacob's parents, counselor, and coach agreed to first work on his fear of striking out; if they could resolve this, Jacob felt he might be able to accept not being first at bat. He enjoyed fooling around with swimming "noodles" and playing balloon hockey and baseball with his father in the basement, so they planned to practice exaggerated, playful "STEEE-RIKE" calls and work up to the point of both Jacob and his father striking out on purpose often.

STRIKING OUT ON PURPOSE IN BASEBALL VIDEO GAME

They also had video games of baseball and his father would practice that way with him, taking turns striking out on purpose. If this was upsetting for Jacob they would begin with non-sports play, using cards or even tossing items into the trash (e.g. orange peels) or sponges into the sink, and missing baskets or making the target, using the words "STRIKE ONE...," and counting up to three strikes, to get Jacob comfortable and playful with this sequence in activities with no anxiety.

WATCHING VIDEOS OF FAMOUS PLAYERS STRIKING OUT

Jacob's father found a collection of strike out videos.

DISNEY CHARACTERS WANTING TO BE FIRST AND STRIKING OUT

Jacob still enjoyed playing with Disney characters. His father would set them up to play baseball and have them pretend to argue over who was going to bat first. He would also have them strike out and get really upset and see if Jacob would want to reassure them or have them reassure each other. He would add playfulness to this demonstration and see if Jacob would want to join in.

WATCHING FUNNY STRIKE OUT VIDEOS

Jacob's father also found some funny striking out videos a group of kids had made. He screened them to pick out and download ones that he thought Jacob would enjoy.

STRIKING OUT ON PURPOSE IN BACKYARD BASEBALL

Jacob and his father often practiced hitting and catching in the backyard too. His father would practice striking out during those unpressured practices, using the silly, playful tone they had established from the previous activities.

ADDING IN REAL TEAMMATES

Jacob and his parents invited over a few of his teammates for an informal baseball game and barbeque and got them to go along with playful, purposeful striking out. At first they thought it was ridiculous, as they were used to trying as hard as they could to hit the ball, but soon they too found it fun. While they said, "We're not really going to do this at real games," they seemed happy to get "permission" to strike out and be silly. Most children (and probably a lot of professional baseball players) have a fear of striking out; they have just developed more adaptive ways of coping than Jacob had. So just about everybody could relate to Jacob's phobia, and perhaps they too also benefited from this playful practice. Once enough of Jacob's teammates were at his house, they could also have a mini-practice where they would try to hit the ball. It would also present an opportunity do some experimenting with the line-up—and to see if Jacob could accept not being first at bat.

Losing the game

They went through a similar series of activities, this time instead of practicing striking out, they practiced losing.

LOSING IN PLAYFUL MADE UP GAMES

At home they also planned to practice losing some simple board and card games and some other made-up games to increase his exposures. They would take turns purposely being The Losing Team, even giving it an acronym name, TLT, as Jacob loved acronyms and secret codes. "Who gets to be TLT this time?" his father would call out, and he could pretend to compete against Jacob, to be TLT every time.

WATCHING THE ENDS OF RECORDED BASEBALL GAMES

Jacob's parents set up the TV to record just about every baseball game they could find on the schedule and together they would watch the ends of many baseball games, with Jacob's father pointing out how the players on the TLT were reacting. Some of them clearly reacted with anger, frustration, and disappointment, even though they stuck around with their teammates, shook hands with the opposing team and didn't stomp off or yell... usually. Watching the pros gave Jacob lots of exposure to losing and losers; he often felt frustrated, too, especially when he thought the umpire made a terrible call. Interestingly, he really noticed (and didn't approve) when a player with a bad attitude or the manager showed poor sportsmanship.

PRACTICING WITH PEERS

Ms. West worked on the components of worrying about feeling blamed by his teammates for striking out or losing. Jacob participated in a social skills group she organized, which included playing fast-paced games that involved only luck, rather than requiring skill or strategy. She found some old, plastic Disney characters and planned to assign the group the task of making up a simple game in which everyone supports The Loser. She was going to have the group decide on which characters were the winners for each round and they would then pick tokens out of a bag with their eyes closed. Ms. West would make it fun, voicing all the different Disney characters, pretending they were getting upset, and then as a group, composing a congratulatory group chant as a reward for The Loser. She had all kinds of creative ideas to desensitize Jacob— and all the other students in her group, many of whom also had difficulty with losing and similar issues, such as not getting the best grade in the class and not having perfect attendance.

Step 4. Proceed through the levels described in Step 2, combined with anxiety-reducing strategies from Step 3

After a few weeks of participating in these activities with his parents, Ms. West and his social group, and some of the guys on his baseball team, Jacob felt ready for prime time: he wanted to tackle going to a real baseball practice again, but this time already suited up in his uniform and joining the team at practice. He was able to sit through the coach's initial talk, having studied the chart the night before. He also was much less anxious, as his preoccupation with and fears about striking out and losing were less intense. He hadn't experienced either at practice, but he had certainly "practiced" both in different settings, many times over, and he truly felt that while it might not be fun, it wouldn't be "the worst thing in the world if I struck out or we lost a game." Also, listening to and participating in the congratulatory chants with his peers in the social group, he was more comfortable knowing that the loser wouldn't be blamed for everything that went wrong.

Not being first at bat continued to bother Jacob, but only a little. He was so focused on supporting his teammates and trying to be a good "loser" that he didn't always pay attention when the coach went over the batting order.

Summary

Jacob gradually became more comfortable with the reality that sometimes his team would win and sometimes they would lose. After all, no professional team won every game of the season, and lots of great players strike out; their teammates don't get mad at them; and some even make it into the Hall of Fame. He would still worry about it a bit before the real games, but not at practice. The first time he actually did strike out, nothing bad happened, and in fact, the player who followed him struck out too. This made a huge difference in alleviating his worries. Playing second base became a non-issue. He announced he would play whichever position would help his team the most. The more he enjoyed baseball, the happier he was during practice, and this in turn also reduced his anxiety overall. A few weeks later, he was able to join in the locker room, arriving with most of his uniform on so he wouldn't have to get dressed and organize his belongings, participating in the all the jocularity that precedes every practice—and he did this happily, with dramatically reduced anxiety.

CHAPTER 9

TREATING LI'S PHOBIA OF CLOWNS, MASCOTS, AND PEOPLE IN COSTUMES

To him who is in fear everything rustles.
SOPHOCLES

Background

Li is a 14-year-old girl with ASD who talks a little, mostly to request things. She also knows the words to many songs and loves to sing. She is usually happy, although it is difficult to engage with her for more than a few minutes of singing, and sometimes gross motor play like swinging and playing chase.

Li is usually cooperative and well-behaved at school and home, and she follows the rules in both settings for routine tasks and activities, such as eating, dressing, and putting her belongings in the proper place. Although she is not easily bothered by changes in schedule or the arrival of a substitute teacher or new classroom aide, she has one phobia: she becomes terrified when she sees clowns or people in costume. She is especially terrified of the middle-school mascot, the Jolly Green Monster, who always shows up at every sporting event, at pep rallies and sometimes at random times. This amuses and delights everyone... except Li. When she sees the mascot or someone else in costume—at a mall or outside a theater at a movie premier, she completely breaks down in tears, often shaking and screaming, and she always tries to run away.

Although her school team and family have successfully kept her away from events at which the Jolly Green Monster is likely to appear, he seems to pop up everywhere. Along with all the sports trophies, there is Giant Green Monster mask in the glass showcase just inside the entrance to the school. Every day when Li arrives, she slows down and sometimes needs adult help to walk by, always covering her face and breathing rapidly. She often meets one of her assistants at the side door in order to avoid a traumatic start to her day, although it isn't always possible. On special sports days and holidays, the school has many traditions, not surprisingly, that involve the mascot, including a visit to every classroom by a very animated and enthusiastic student dressed up as the Jolly Green Monster. At assemblies and special programs, the Monster also serves as the MC. And on days when there is a big game, many of the local stores prominently display a Jolly Green Mask in their windows.

Haunted by Halloween

Halloween and the weeks leading up to it are also very scary and stressful for Li. Her parents have to run interference, keeping her home from school on dress-up days and away from the art exhibits in the hallways featuring skeletons, ghosts, and every superhero imaginable. They also have to case the community so they can locate and then avoid the pop-up costume stores. Ironically, her community celebrates Halloween in a big way; even the bank tellers and grocery store clerks dress up, so Halloween is truly a nightmare for Li and her family.

Clowns no laughing matter

Li is also terrified of clowns. She was in the hospital to have her tonsils out, which paled in comparison to the terror she felt when a well-meaning doctor dressed like a clown strutted into her room, allegedly to cheer her up. After that, her parents put a sign on her door, apologizing and asking the clown to "please perform for other patients." Of course they avoid the circus or anything like it. Then there are some events that Li would greatly enjoy and that her parents anticipate will be safe (e.g. nobody in costume) only to discover, when the curtain goes up, that everyone is dressed up like an animal or some kind of mythological creature.

Li's parents and teacher have tried to figure out why she has this group of fears. They think maybe she is uncomfortable with the ambiguity of someone in costume and wondering, "Is it real or not? Is that a person or an animal?" Her teachers have tried bringing in the mask from the school's exhibit case to the classroom. But as soon as Li saw it she screamed and headed for the door. She didn't calm down until she saw her teacher place it back in the case and lock it. For days, though, she continued to check under the teacher's desk, to make sure it didn't make its way back to the class. The phobia was beginning to spread; she feared it might materialize in her classroom at any time without warning.

Step 1. Identify key trigger components of the feared object or situation: "Unbundle" the phobia

Li's parents and teachers had trouble thinking of how to unbundle her mask and costume phobia, since she seemed so terrified by anything remotely to do with them. Interestingly, she was not afraid of dolls, although she had never shown much interest in them. She didn't play house or do any kind of pretend play. So perhaps she wasn't afraid of symbolic faces in this "non-masked" form. But this also meant that using dolls in her treatment plan—to help her get more comfortable with masks—might not resonate with Li. She did like stuffed animals, especially a few bears and bunnies she kept in her bed. Although she didn't pretend with them, she liked to hold them and was comforted by rubbing their soft, fuzzy fur.

Scarves not scary

One day her mother was reorganizing her drawers and began playing around with her silky scarves with Li, who liked their soft slithery feel, especially when her mother wrapped them around her arms. Her mother had an idea: She could wrap the scarf around her own face, sort of like a mask, and then pull it off right away. Since Li already loved the scarves and their play routine, maybe that wouldn't be scary. She began to think creatively about other ways to work with the mask/costume trigger, using the scarves or other scarf-like things.

They came up with the following list of issues that they suspected were likely components of her phobia, starting with these five, which might lead them to other possibilities or down other paths:

1. The sight of a person, but not seeing their actual face.

2. The sight of an unreal/pretend face (mask).

3. The sight of a face with "distortions" as in a clown's face.

4. The sight of the Jolly Green Monster mascot in all its forms.

5. The sight of clowns.

Step 2. Determine measures that reduce the child's anxiety: Self-regulating strategies

Li felt happy and relaxed when she was playing on her own, especially when singing her favorite songs to herself. Her play often seemed aimless to others; she moved objects around, rearranged them or filled up containers with various toys and dumped them out. She also liked to swing and could do this for a long time. At school she took "swinging breaks" in the OT room, and at home the family installed one swing outside and another in the basement. Li enjoyed coloring with markers too. She often picked bright colors, drew designs on brightly colored construction paper; cut up the paper with scissors; and glued down the pieces to make designs and collages. Her art wasn't representational, although it was colorful and interesting. That is, her parents and teachers didn't think she was drawing a particular object, person or place. However, she could concentrate on her collages for a long time, perhaps up to an hour, and the activity was both engaging and soothing for her.

Li also liked snuggling in her quilt on her bed with her stuffed animals. Sometimes she would run to her bed during the day for a quick snuggle. However, her parents tried to limit this to the night, as they didn't like the idea of her withdrawing into her room by herself.

Co-regulating strategies

There were a few activities Li enjoyed doing with her parents. These included playing with soft blankets, clothing or fabric, like her mother's scarves. She really enjoyed twirling around with them and singing. She also liked it when they pushed her on the swing, never tiring and sometimes asking to "Go faster!"

Step 3. Design levels of gradually increasing exposure to each component

1. The sight of a person without being able to see their actual face

Li's parents and teachers weren't really sure what aspect of this component was scary so they did some experimenting. Her mother tried covering up her face with a scarf and Li looked up, noticing quickly, and immediately pulled the scarf away, but didn't look distressed. So this might be a good place to start, with something that piqued her interest but wasn't scary and was related to this component of her fear. They made the following list of initial steps:

— Covering up each other's faces with scarves gently and playfully.

— Covering up each other's faces with blankets when they were cuddling on Li's bed.

2. The sight of a "pretend" face (mask)
The family added these steps, including creating a "pseudo-mask" out of the scarves, and incorporate it into their play:

— Buying some inexpensive scarves made from textured fabric Li liked and cutting eyeholes in them. (Li's mother was willing to try just about anything but drew the line at cutting up her designer scarves!), and then playfully covering/uncovering each other's faces. Variations:

 – Make this a turn-taking, peek-a-boo game.

 – Incorporate stuffed animals and cover up their faces.

— If she got used to the eyeholes, add mouth holes in the scarves and repeat the above steps.

— If this went smoothly, cut some scarves up in face shapes, making them more and more mask-like, eventually even adding a string in the back so they would stay in place on their own or on the stuffed animals' heads.

— If this continued to go smoothly, enlist the help of her teachers in making paper masks at school with familiar arts and crafts materials such as colored paper, markers and glue, and sticky-backed plastic eyes; glue the masks to popsicle sticks so they could be used as simple puppets, popping up quickly and then hiding and placing them gradually closer to Li as tolerated.

3. The sight of a face with distortions as in a clown's face
Li's parents recalled how distressed she became if they—or anyone—had food on their faces. She also shied away from anyone wearing make-up, although she liked to watch her mother put on lipstick, so that might be a reasonable place to start. They came up with the following steps:

— Watching Li's mother put on lipstick and offering to put lipstick on Li.

— Li's mother "misses" and gets lipstick on her cheeks.

— Putting lipstick on Li in the mirror and "missing" and getting it on her face; continue, as long as Li does not find this distressing. (Ideally, she will find it interesting and entertaining.)

— Applying make-up with face painting crayons as a special group activity at school.

— Continue with face painting at school (adults first, then involve students, including Li), more closely approximating a clown's face, as Li can tolerate.

— Watching video clips of clowns putting on their make-up.

— Finding stills of clown faces on the internet to look at, print out and cut out.

— Watching video clips of clowns.

4. The sight of the specific Jolly Green
Monster mascot in all its forms
While this was the most frequently encountered problem, Li's parents and teachers decided to work on the steps first, hoping that once she was able to tolerate, even enjoy the activities without distress, she would be more willing to face the dreaded Green Monster. They came up with the following steps:

— Introduce a tiny black and white image of the mascot, the size of a postage stamp.

  – If accepted, cut out several for her to color green.

  – If not, her teacher can draw a rough sketch that approximates, but not too closely, the face of the mascot, coloring it green and then moving on to a more realistic mascot face.

— Print out a small photograph of the mascot, then increasingly larger ones.

— Eventually, both at school and at home, cut out eye and mouth holes. Glue masks to sticks, as they had done previously with the scarves.

— Make paper-maché masks at school, moving from simple, less anxiety-producing ones to closer likenesses of the Jolly Green Monster.

— Make a video with a phone camera of Li entering the school through the front door into the lobby, such that the mask could be seen in the distance. Sing one of Li's favorite songs in the video and then watch the video with Li.

— Make another simple video featuring a close-up of the mask and watch it with Li.

— Purchase some new pajamas that are as similar as possible to the Green Monster's costume, which resembles green fuzzy pajamas.

— Give Li the opportunity to wear the pajamas to bed for several nights.

— Schedule and celebrate "Pajama Day" at school, as a special treat so Li can wear her new green pajamas.

Step 4. Proceed through the Levels described in Step 2, combined with anxiety reducing strategies from Step 3

Li, her parents and teachers worked through the steps above. Li enjoyed playing with the scarves in a modified game of peek-a-boo. When they added the eyeholes she was nervous at first, but soon relaxed and enjoyed this variation too. Adding the mouth had the same initial effect; she was nervous at first but then joined in, feeling less threatened with the gradual exposure. Li's father jumped in and took some videos, as they were having so much fun, and Li watched them over and over, not realizing that she was desensitizing herself to masks in the process!

Li also enjoyed making masks at school. Interestingly she didn't push them away when her classmates held them up; perhaps she was getting used to this kind of play. Or perhaps she recognized her classmates' clothes or their faces under the masks.

The activities involving lipstick and then face paint were also successful. But one day her mother painted her own face without Li's knowledge or participation, which frightened her. She began wiping her mother's face and started to cry. Her mother quickly removed it and took her outside immediately for an extended break on the swing. Since Li returned to a calm state and since she had the face paints in her pocket, she put a dot of red on Li's lips each time she gave her a push. Then she encouraged Li to reciprocate and dot her lips. She added several colors, so both their faces were peppered with a whole rainbow of dots, which certainly would have been scary if Li had come face to face with her suddenly. But swinging was so relaxing that she enjoyed the activity far more than expected, even though her mother looked like she was coming down with some rare and dreadful disease!

They continued to play, with her mother stopping from time to time and adding some paint so she would look more clown-like.

This gradual transformation did not cause Li any distress so they continued, with her mother taking pictures to show Li later on.

Send in the clowns

Her mother soon felt she was ready to watch the videos of the clown putting on make-up. But when she turned it on Li screamed and ran out of the room. Li's mother back pedaled a little and printed out still photos of a clown putting on make-up with face paint very much like what they had used, and Li became more intrigued— and less scared. She enlarged the pictures and posted them on the computer screen a few days later just before introducing the video again. Li approached the computer and then backed off, saying "NO NO NO," so her mother immediately stopped the video and covered the screen with her hands. Li approached the screen again and tried to get a peek at the image.

Hide and seek

Li, like most children, seemed both drawn to and afraid of looking. Her mother playfully turned this into an "approach-avoidance" game, covering the screen saying "NO!" while hiding the image and then saying "NOW PEEK," while uncovering and then quickly covering it up. Gradually Li got used to and actually enjoyed this game. Once she got through the entire video, she wanted to watch it over and over. Her teacher found a similar video at school and the whole class watched it before then putting on their own face paint in art.

By this time Li was also happily coloring the postage stamp-sized pictures of the school mascot. She then moved on to cutting out and making masks out of larger pictures. She had come a long way in a few weeks! She also began to enjoy watching the video of her teacher arriving at school, singing Li's favorite song. And after watching it five, six or seven or more times, she starting looking for—and looking at—the mascot mask in the glass case. Seizing the moment, her teacher took her for a walk past the case, but Li was not yet ready for the real thing. She covered her eyes and started to cry when she spotted the creepy creature. So a few more videos and few more monster close-ups later, Li slowly began to tolerate it. The addition of singing silly songs, including Li's favorite tune, contributed to her comfort level.

Not easy being green

At home, her mother, somewhat reluctantly, began dressing up in a fuzzy green costume she borrowed from school. She experimented with it, putting it in a pile with the scarves on the floor. Although it didn't scare her, Li took matters into her own hands and threw it in the trash! This gave her mother a new idea. She pulled it out of the trash and put it on the table in the playroom. Li picked it up again and carried it to the trash. Her mother followed her, pulled it out and put it on the sofa. And she put the trashcan in the middle of the room and continued the game, hiding it under the rug, behind the couch, and even in the refrigerator. Each time Li would find it and put it in the trash. This continued until both of them were in hysterics. Each time the costume appeared Li was getting increasing exposure to it without feeling anxious, which was precisely the goal.

Her mother expanded the game. She pulled out a quilt and invited Li to come and cuddle with her on the sofa, a comforting activity. She then pulled in the costume to join them and Li cuddled up with the fuzzy, green, now-not-so-scary costume too. Her mother then tossed it into the trash and in a reversal of roles, Li laughed, fished it out of the trash and brought her new-found, previously frightening "friend" back to the sofa to cuddle with them!

Soon her mother slowly stepped into the costume. Before she pulled it over her entire body, she went to get Li's green pajamas so the two of them could play dress-up together in a fun, non-threatening way. She switched on Li's favorite CD and they danced around together, laughing, singing…and green. Her mother added the paper cut-out mask to their costumes and Li continued to dance around cheerfully. Her mother took a few pictures and emailed them to Li's teacher, who brought them out and looked at them with Li and her classmates the following day at school.

Her teacher then took a giant leap and brought in the once-feared mascot mask to show the class and Li looked up inquisitively, but not fearfully. Then she pushed even further, holding up the mask and putting on the costume; Li and her classmates laughed and joined in singing the ABCs with the teacher adding in the word, "Green Monster" here and there to add to the humor ("ABCDEF… Green monster…").

Summary

Li, her parents, and teachers enjoyed going through these steps, as cumbersome (sometimes) and as far-fetched (sometimes) as they seemed. Although she was initially afraid, she was also intrigued. The masks, costumes, and make-up were meaningful to her even though they had caused her anxiety. After all this practice, which took place over a few months, Li became comfortable coming in the front door of her school, often stopping to look at the mascot mask. She continued to be afraid when the Green Monster showed up unexpectedly in her classroom or when she spotted him at a new gas station opening, although she no longer panicked. But small likenesses and souvenir masks she came across in stores no longer set off any emotional alarms. Seeing clowns at a distance no longer elicited any fear, but she rapidly retreated when they approached her.

On several occasions, she startled, screamed, and tried to run away when she unexpectedly encountered people in costumes, for example, once at a county fair and another time at a Presidents' Day assembly at school. However, her parents and school team decided they would start working in a similar way on Halloween masks, beginning the first week of school in September. They anticipated that the process would go more quickly now that many of her extreme, fearful reactions were behind her.

CHAPTER 10

TREATING JORDAN'S PHOBIA OF BEING LATE

Background

Jordan is a seven-year-old boy with ASD who has become quite communicative and social in his own way with adults, although still not with peers. He has gone through phases of different fears, first of more concrete things like new places or changes in the position or location of furniture at home. Over the past year, possibly as a result of a greater understanding of the concept of time and more scheduled events, he has become increasingly worried about being late. This includes being late to school, therapy appointments, playdates and other social events. He also worries he will miss the school bus, both in the morning and afternoon, and he thinks about it all day at school. And he worries about other people being late, too, like when his parents invite friends or relatives over for dinner. As the time approaches his anxiety ramps up and he gets irritable, even angry. He may stand outside his mother's bedroom door, bothering her every few seconds, telling her what time it is and reminding her that, "We have to hurry up!" Or he may bark orders at his classmates and repeating, "You'll be late and ruin everything!" He insists on arriving early for each activity and becomes anxious and irritable as the time approaches. On occasion he hits the people around him out of distress. Once he was so anxious about getting to the train station, that his father forgot his suitcase and had to return home to get it. They actually did miss their train that time. And another time his family arrived at the airport so early, their plane was sitting on the runway... 400 miles away at its original point of departure!

Step 1. Identify key trigger components of the feared object or situation: "Unbundle" the phobia

Jordan's fears about being late causes problems for him, his entire family, his classmates, and anyone who has to be somewhere with him at a certain time. His school team decides to collaborate with his family in tackling this problem. They meet and try to identify the various components that seem to be involved. They know he prefers to get to activities before they begin, probably, they suspect, so he can get organized and mentally run through everything he's supposed to do. They also know he gets upset if he misses an activity; and he often says, "We can't be late or we'll miss the whole thing!"

He loves it when his parents have people over to dinner, but he watches the clock well before their expected time of arrival and worries if they are "fashionably late" and get there even five minutes after the said time. He asks repeatedly as the time approaches if they are still coming, and if maybe they got into an accident or the car ran out of gas. When his aunt and uncle didn't walk in the door at exactly 7 pm for his birthday dinner, he broke down, worrying that they'd been hurt... or "maybe they died." "It is so disruptive and so annoying," says his Mother, "that sometimes it's easier not to invite people over so we don't have to go through this long, agonizing ritual that can go on for hours and hours before they're due to arrive."

Jordan has several very specific worries, such as missing the school bus, that cause him to be very grumpy from the moment he opens his eyes in the morning. After the lunch bell rings he immediately starts watching the clock, ruminating about whether it will be late and whether he'll get out to the bus stop on time. What if he forgets his homework and has to go back and get it and then he misses it? What if the bus leaves a couple of minutes early and he misses it?

His parents and teachers have tried "just about everything." They have explained to him and have had the bus driver explain to him that she will wait for him in the morning, "no matter what," and won't *ever* leave without him at the end of the school day. And, in the unlikely event of his not getting on the bus (nobody dare whisper the word, "miss") his mother would drive him to school in the morning or pick him up in the afternoon. His teacher also tried covering up the clock in the classroom, but this caused him more anxiety, and he ask repeatedly what time it was.

The behavioral consultant to his school program tried a system of rewarding him for not making angry statements about being late. Jordan definitely wanted to earn the rewards, but couldn't stop himself from getting more and more worried, which caused him to become irritable and totally preoccupied, so much so that he stopped paying attention to his school work and missed several important assignments. The behaviorist also suggested having him purposely arrive at the bus stop late with his teacher for a few days, so he could practice. This just increased his agitation and didn't show any signs of diminishing. The magnitude of his baseline anxiety increased, began earlier and he took longer to de-escalate after the reaction.

They came up with the following list of components related to his fear of being late. He worried about the following:

1. If he is late he will miss the event entirely.

2. He will arrive after an activity has already started and he will not know where to go, who to sit with, and what to do.

3. If he misses the bus in the morning his teacher will be angry with him.

4. The bus will leave without him at the end of the day and he'll never get home.

5. If dinner guests don't arrive on time something terrible has happened to them.

6. If houseguests don't arrive on time, they will cancel and he will be disappointed.

Step 2. Determine measures that reduce the child's anxiety: Self-regulating strategies

Jordan liked playing computer games but they often made him more agitated, especially if something didn't go right or the entire game "froze." He didn't have a lot of ways to amuse or soothe himself. Sometimes he liked jumping on his trampoline, and recently he got interested in looking up information about specific topics on the internet such as when Presidents were born and died. He recently found out the President's daily agenda was posted online, and he liked to look up what time the President had to be where. He also liked studying bus and train routes and maps in general, and would spend hours studying them, often asking the adults in his life where they lived and worked and where they went on weekends so he could figure out the fastest and most efficient way to get there.

Co-regulating strategies

Jordan had close relationships with several adults in his life, including his parents, his teaching assistant, his occupational therapist, and the school behaviorist. He always had a "question of the day" for them, which lately related to their modes of transportation and destinations. He had also ferreted out information about the make and model of car each drove, how many songs they had on their iPods and if they had a dog. He greatly enjoyed these conversations even though they could get very repetitive. Whenever he began to get anxious or upset, his parents would masterfully steer the conversation in the direction of one of these topics, which usually captured his interest and he would calm down.

Jordan had a wonderful sense of humor and especially liked playful exaggeration and irony. If he asked how long it had taken his teacher to drive to school and she answered, "Well, there was a huge traffic jam, so it took me, oh, about 103 hours," he burst out laughing, although he would follow up with, "You're just kidding right?" just to be sure. If his father asked him where he wanted to stop for a quick dinner on the way home, "The Taj Mahal," or "the top of the Eiffel Tower" were his first choices. So incorporating humor into the gradual exposure process would probably help.

Step 3. Design levels of gradually increasing exposure to each component

1. Worry that if he is late he will actually miss the event
The family and school decided to work collaboratively with him, first to determine how early he was comfortable arriving at an event, and then gradually decreasing that time by two minutes, then five minutes, etc. eventually arriving a couple of minutes after the appointed time but before the actual activities got underway.

BE LATE FOR HIS OCCUPATIONAL THERAPY SESSION
They worked with his OT to schedule a simple, flexible activity that couldn't actually start until he arrived. She would pretend to be surprised he was late and playfully told him she had to start without him, which he knew was impossible.

2. Be right on time but not early for other activities
They planned to then expand the plan to intentionally arrive exactly on time, giving him more and more practice tolerating this. Then he could choose the next activity he wanted to be on time (but not early) for and would accompany this with anxiety reducing strategies. Regarding the other part of his worry, that is, that if he is late, he will arrive after the activity has started, and then he would not know where to sit, who to sit with, and what to do, they were glad he wanted to do well in his participation and that he knew that getting there on time helped him with this. They knew he worked hard to follow along with the social aspects of group activities and with school and that this was really quite adaptive for him to want to arrive on time, but they also wanted him to know that even if he were late the adults would help him so he would be able to participate successfully. They devised the following:

— Late for OT: So parents talked again first with his OT with whom he was very close and she suggested he arrive late on purpose for her session and she would make a big deal about it playfully and pretend the activity had started and then explain it to him.

— Late for social skills group with lots of advanced help: Jordan's parents talked with his Social Skills group leader and they planned a session to which he would be a few minutes late. They would explain which activities they would be doing, and when he arrived his teacher would make sure he joined the group and participated in the planned activity.

— Late for social skills group with less help: They would repeat the same steps but without previewing the activity with his parents. The teacher would continue to help him join in, however.

— Late for school with planning and support.

3. Worry that if he misses the bus in the morning, he'll arrive at school late and his teacher will be angry with him

While Jordan's parents and teacher had explained to him that his teacher would not be angry and that nobody got in trouble for being late, Jordan had watched too many TV programs and heard from other kids at other schools that, "You can really get in trouble if you're late." So he flat out didn't believe them.

They came up with the following steps:

— Teacher being late: His teacher knew she was going to arrive late one morning so she would make a big deal about it and joke around, first arriving all frazzled in a slapstick way, then asking if he would be angry, and taking a straw poll in the class, asking every single student (for repetition) if they were angry at her.

— Being late once at school, and moving from one class to the next with a teacher's support.

— Being late to school with advanced planning and support.

— Being late to school with less planning.

4. Worry that the bus will leave without him at the end of the day and he won't be able to go home

Jordan's parents and school staff had learned that giving him a wordy explanation would not convince him otherwise. Even practicing caused too much distress. They tried to further unbundle this and make it more manageable, so they agreed on "almost missing the bus" and came up with the following:

— Watch videos of school buses driving away on YouTube with his teacher, who would bring up a hypothetical situation about how maybe somebody could or had missed their bus.

— Make a video with the good-natured bus driver's involvement, of what missing the bus would look like, with the driver waving goodbye and announcing that any kids who weren't there would get picked up by their parents... and then driving off.

— "Miss" the bus at the end of the day, planning ahead of time and having his mother pick him up, combining this with co-regulation activities. He could, for example, chat with his behaviorist and ask as many questions as he wanted about how she got to school, what route she took home, a topic he loved, while watching the bus drive away and waiting for his mother to arrive.

5. Worry that if his parents' dinner guests do not arrive exactly on time, something terrible has happened to them

Jordan's parents had some good friends, the Adlers, who would be perfect for this kind of practice, since Mr. Adler was a real prankster and had always had a special relationship with Jordan. He would be good at working in a lot of playful exaggeration into the practice activities later on. They came up with the following steps:

— Have the Adlers pretend they are going to be late but actually arrive on time: Mr. Adler could call, going on and on and telling Jordan about how late they might be, using a lot of co-regulating humor.

— Have the Adlers arrive late but with plenty of warning and co-regulating use of playful exaggeration.

— The Adlers arrive a little late without warning.

6. Worry that if people don't arrive on time, they will cancel and not show up at all and he will be very disappointed

Jordan's parents had mixed feelings about working on this issue since Jordan truly enjoyed having company. They thought it was a positive quality that he was disappointed when guests cancelled, that he, as a child with ASD was able to form such strong attachments and express such deep emotions. While they didn't want him to have a big meltdown, they did feel strongly as did his teachers that learning to tolerate similar disappointments was in his best interests—and the family's.

Jordan's parents developed back-up plans in the past, "Just in case they don't come." Sometimes this was helpful, although often Jordan would obsess about it, but nobody had ever cancelled at the last minute. As they were thinking this through his parents thought maybe that's why he was so anxious about the possibility. He hadn't ever experienced a "last minute cancellation." This gave them a couple of ideas:

— Invite the Adlers over with Jordan's knowledge. They would call and cancel at the last minute, but there would be a back-up plan in place: Jordan could go out to his favorite burger joint for dinner. While this might sound silly to some people, it seemed very reasonable to them, and the Adlers were willing to go along.

— If that went well: Plan with the Adlers that they "*might*" come over and have a back-up plan, with them cancelling at the last minute.

Step 4. Proceed through the levels described in Step 2, combined with anxiety reducing strategies from Step 3

As they already knew, Jordan wouldn't be able to tolerate practicing being late in any form without increasing his agitation, asking repeated questions and experiencing a high level of anxiety, unless the adults did a good job putting anxiety reduction measures in place at the same time. "Planned" late practice helped him a bit, as he knew it wouldn't really result in missing something, but it was still very upsetting for him. His friend, the school behaviorist, who was especially playful tried several variations of timed games, using the timer setting on her phone, to help reduce his anxiety. They did some role play, pretending they were President and Mrs. Obama running late for his lunch with the Secretary of State, which Jordan thought was hilarious, even though he needed to make sure that it was, "Just a joke, right?" He also found the quacking sound on her phone especially funny, as her own son had set her text tone, unbeknownst to her, surprising them both one day with loud quacking, sending him into fits of laughter which still happened at the very mention of the incident. She set her timer to quack at two-minute intervals so that when they were practicing waiting for something, this would make him laugh, reducing his anxiety. Armed with this presidential role play practice and the quacking timer, the behaviorist and teacher together helped Jordan through several steps of practicing being late for class and the bus, planning ahead each time.

All was going well; Jordan began to tolerate being late for school and for class; and expressed worry less frequently. But his worrying about being late for the bus at the end of the day continued, and their efforts to practice, with his mother coming and with the videos although fun for him, hadn't eliminated his anxiety.

Nobody was sure why this was lingering, as he did not appear worried when class ended and he could actually see that the bus was there. They decided to add a step of playful, funny role play right after lunch about missing the bus, thinking this could work as a "booster shot" to bring his anxiety down as he moved through the afternoon.

The behaviorist agreed to meet him at recess and invite Jordan and some of his classmates to play "The President is late for lunch again." They found some takers, who added in different variations, like "The Principal is late for the parent meeting," and "Their Parents' Bosses are late for work," catching on to the idea of authority figures being late once in a while too. One child said what if SpongeBob was late (which could have been a real episode) so they played this out with their own silly variations. This dramatic role play around late themes clearly reduced Jordan's anxiety through the afternoon.

Summary

Jordan's anxiety subsided quite substantially as a result of the steps his parents and school team had taken and everyone felt good about his progress. He still became distressed around being late if he was going to a new activity; he already had increased anxiety, understandably, and was naturally nervous about understanding who would be there and what was going to happen. He became worried about the bus again when a new driver took over, but after a few days that subsided. He also would become anxious and agitated if several upsetting things happened in a row. One week, a virus spread around the school and several special events and activities had to be cancelled. Jordan himself ended up getting sick and became more irritable and anxious. The behaviorist did some extra fun role play practice sessions, and once this schedule and his health returned to normal, his anxiety decreased too.

CHAPTER 11

COLLABORATING WITH OTHERS

Treating phobias can sometimes be relatively straightforward and require only a few play sessions with a parent. More often, however, it is more complicated, requiring the implementation of multiple steps and processes. It can be very useful to involve several people in the process.

Enlisting the help of people who have some connection to when/ where the phobia trigger occurs makes it easier for the child to generalize their emerging comfort with the elements of the trigger situation to the actual situation. We have treated many children for phobias around thunderstorms, yet there has never been a real thunderstorm during treatment. Parents usually work closely with us in the office so that they can work on components of the process at home, where the child is more likely to be during a storm and more likely to be with them. It will also be key to carry over some components to the school setting, so the child will become able to generalize to that environment and that group of people.

Sometimes the key people involved in the trigger situation, such as the doctor or dentist, the ambulance driver or lab technician, can be only minimally involved. Others can and then stand in through role play, pretend, simulation, costumes, and manipulating dolls and toy figures.

Sometimes the key people may not be adept at doing the activities involved in desensitizing the child. This may be due to time constraints or their own comfort level with the issue or with the child in a particular situation. For example, sometimes it is so stressful for parents to even contemplate their child becoming distressed, that they aren't able to stay relaxed and playful during gradual exposure. In such circumstances, someone else may be more effective, even though the parent may be the primary comfort and support person once they encounter the actual trigger situation. This can generally work effectively if the someone else doing the desensitizing steps can work with the parents as much as possible even if the parent isn't comfortable taking the lead.

Another person, such as a grandparent or uncle, therapist or babysitter, could take the lead. Ideally, this person would have a close relationship with the child but would not get stressed by this process. It doesn't matter who takes the lead, as long as they are skilled at working with the child, understand the model and goals, and can work respectfully with the parents and other key people involved in the trigger situation.

If a school event or setting is the trigger, enlisting the help of the child's teacher, aid, and therapists will probably contribute to greater success. The teacher can help the child with a phobia about making mistakes on classwork, for example. However if the school team is not open to this kind of treatment or is not able to do it effectively, one can also work on the issues outside of the school environment. Parents or outside therapists can work on phobias around making mistakes on homework, getting hard worksheets, being late to class, changes in schedule, etc. Even if school staff are not directly involved in the treatment process, letting major school personnel know you are working on these issues outside of school can help increase understanding of and compassion towards the child.

Collaborating with occupational and speech therapists

Collaborating with a child's occupational therapist can help with phobias that have a sensory component (sound, touch, smell, motion). A child may have occupational therapy through school or privately through health insurance, for fine motor issues, for support in self-help/daily living skills, or for sensory integration/ regulation. Often when we present this model, people will suggest that sensory integration could also be used to treat heightened reactions to sensory experiences. We hypothesize that while many of the phobia triggers were initially based in sensory overload of some sort, and many still have a sensory component, the child's intense responses have evolved and now "have a life of their own" and affect the child emotionally in addition to the initial sensory overload.

This may explain, in part, the anticipatory anxiety and the intensity and duration of distress. Becoming upset by injections, startled and shaken up for a moment upon hearing the siren of an ambulance, or feeling disgusted by touching something slimy are quite common, and even more so in children who have diminished capacity to cope with intense sensory experiences. Treating these issues from a sensory perspective, as occupational therapists and others often do, can be highly effective. Treating the total experiences as we describe in our model, in conjunction with people familiar with how the sensory system processes, is often a very helpful combination. Often OTs are experienced and clever at generating small steps with a sensory component, contributing to the gradual exposure process.

Sometimes professionals and others working with the child try to avoid sensory input, so the child will not experience discomfort or distress, which is certainly laudable. We have seen children sitting through lunch in the cafeteria, assemblies, recess, and even in the classroom, wearing different types of headphones, from the tiniest earbuds to large, "industrial strength" apparatus. This may be the only way the child can cope with these situations and still participate in learning. This isn't the only solution, however, although it is a good interim measure while various steps for gradual exposure are being worked on. The problem with tuning out too much auditory input is that the child misses experiences they might enjoy or learn from, and they can become more socially isolated, so addressing such issues in collaboration with an OT can be highly beneficial.

Collaborating with a child's speech therapist can also help. A child may have speech therapy through school and/or privately. Using pretend play, role play, making videos, or story-telling about the child's intense experiences related to their phobias are within the expertise and focus of many speech therapists.

For phobias related to food and eating, experienced speech and occupational therapists who specialize in feeding often work collaboratively, with medical specialists such as a nurse. There are also feeding teams, both hospital-based and private, who specialize in working with parents and children around food-related fears.

Putting phobia treatment goals and processes into the child's Individualized Education Plan (IEP)

There are many different ways of incorporating work on phobias into children's IEPs. How to do this depends on the phobia and what it impacts. Many phobias affect a child's capacity to access various aspects of the curriculum, such a fears of the cafeteria, gym buzzers, performing or even watching performances in the auditorium. Other phobias may influence a child's capacity to participate in any number of learning and social experiences. We worked with a child who had an intense phobia about losing in games, and the math curriculum was taught through competitions and games. Another child had intense fear of missing his school bus at the end of the day, causing him to be distracted throughout the afternoon, resulting in him missing much of his afternoon curriculum. One child had an intense fear of masks and statues, and especially the school mascot mask, on display in the main lobby. She also feared people dressed in costumes, causing her frequent distress and limiting access to many school events and celebrations. Treatment for these phobias can be incorporated into the child's IEP in various categories, depending on the phobia's impact and the plan to treat it and/or develop ways to work around it. See examples below.

IEP section	Explanation/ rationale	Example
Student Profile	Document anxiety in narrative form to reduce interpretations of associated behaviors and actions.	Eva has been diagnosed with (autism) and anxiety (Dr. Fear, 2010, see file). Eva has fears of making mistakes, thunderstorms, and being in busy community spaces where students gather, such as the cafeteria.
		Eva's inability to manage/cope with her anxiety may appear as avoidance, disrespect, or inappropriate behavior.

The fact that the child has anxiety and specific phobias can be included in the Student Profile section of the IEP, with a brief description of how it manifests throughout the child's day. This can be helpful in creating an atmosphere of supporting, rather than blaming the child for behaviors that may be confusing or appear to be willfully non-compliant, such as hiding under a desk during a storm or running out of a noisy cafeteria.

How the child's anxiety limits their access to academic and non-academic aspects of their school experience is key both for understanding the child and also to justify accommodations, modifications and treatment. Below is an example of how this can be included in the child's IEP:

Current performance	Document how anxiety limits the student's access to the general curriculum/ school community.	ACADEMIC: Eva's anxiety affects progress in the curricular areas in a variety of ways. Anxiety often prevents her from participating in group work in academic classes given her fear of making mistakes, which is magnified within small groups. Eva often finds ways to leave the classroom, such as asking to see the nurse, going to her locker, or to the bathroom when group work is assigned.
		NON-ACADEMIC: Eva's anxiety affects progress in areas of other educational needs, such as participation in the school community, socialization, and communication.
		For example, Eva is unable to attend school-wide assemblies, and cannot eat lunch in the cafeteria. This significantly limits her ability to participate in the school community with peers, which in turn affects her ability to initiate, manage and sustain peer relationships.

One can write in specific, reasonable measures that need to be taken, called "accommodations," to help the child cope given their anxiety, such as the following:

Accommodations	Document the supports which, when provided to the student, assist them in achieving the same goal as their typical peers.	– Warnings prior to fire drills when possible. – Breaks with assistant or therapist during thunderstorms. – Opportunities for breaks during the day in a designated, semi-personal space.

Many children with anxiety need modifications to their program so they can sustain a sufficiently regulated state for participating and learning. Often while one is working on an issue, such as helping a child become able to eat in the cafeteria, modifications such as lunch with a small group in a small space for this purpose is warranted, even if the ultimate goal is for the child to be comfortable eating in the cafeteria. Like other components of an IEP, what modifications are needed can change as a child's needs change and as their anxiety diminishes. Below are examples of some specific modifications in a child's IEP due to the impact of their anxiety:

Modifications	Document the supports that are necessary for the student to participate but which significantly change the intended outcome of the activity or action.	– Non-attendance at school-wide assemblies. – Provided with a daily transcript of morning announcements. – Lunch in a smaller physical space.

Some children need what are called "supplementary aids and services," which include a range of external supports, that can help with anxiety, such as wearing earbuds to listen to music during times of high stress. Below are some examples of putting this in the child's IEP:

Supplementary aids and services	Supplementary aids and services are supports provided to "enable students with disabilities to be educated with nondisabled children to the maximum extent appropriate" (Individuals with Disabilities Education Act, § 300.42)	– Use of earbuds during storms to reduce noise. – Use of a small fidget toy during mathematics class.

Work on treating specific phobias as well as generalized anxiety can then be more directly identified in the body of the IEP, under the child's Annual Goals.

Annual goals	Document how anxiety is addressed in school to make it a living part of educational work.	Eva will develop and utilize three co-regulation strategies with the teacher or assistant during morning announcements.

Additionally, treatment goals around specific phobias impacting school participation can be included within the annual goals and benchmarks of individual therapists, including occupational therapy and speech therapy. Behavioral and counseling IEP goals can target treatment and progress related to anxiety and phobias.

Collaborating with mental health providers

Working with a mental health provider, such as a Licensed Mental Health Counselor (LMHC), a Licensed Social Worker (LICSW), a Psychologist or a Psychiatrist experienced in treating children with anxiety and phobias and ideally, children who are like your child, can be helpful. This person can guide the treatment process and be a consultant when the process gets stuck.

Therapists who are experienced in play therapy are often open to this kind of model. Some therapists experienced in cognitive behavioral therapy who work with young children may also be open to this model or use similar techniques. Unfortunately such professionals are not always available through school, covered by your health insurance or close to where you live. Sometimes only a few sessions are needed to treat simple phobias, while for some children who have ongoing phobias and an overall elevated baseline of anxiety, ongoing treatment can be most effective. If you are able to find and work with one of these professionals, having them work in conjunction with others in the child's life, including parents and teachers, is especially effective. Working in isolation with the child is less likely to lead to ongoing generalized change for young children or less verbal children than working in close collaboration with other primary people in the child's life, who they encounter, work with, play with, and live with every day.

Collaborating with behavior specialists

Working to alleviate phobias is often taken on by behavior specialists who may be on the child's school or home-based team or who may provide consultation to the family or educational team. Behavior therapists may be BCBAs (Board Certified Behavior Analysts) or have a background and training in using positive approaches to support a child in behavior change. Some behavior therapists have training related to the model we describe in this book and will be helpful in developing and implementing these and other effective strategies. Others focus more exclusively on "problem behaviors" and frame their work more within the immediate context of an overt problem. They work toward changing observable, socially relevant behaviors largely through applying the principles of learning theory.

Some professionals, including some behavior therapists, do not have a background or training in anxiety disorders and may misinterpret intense responses that are anxiety driven as willful misbehavior, viewing these behaviors as they would a child reaching for a cookie, then looking at you and smiling after you have said, "No cookies." Some professionals have training in working with children with developmental disabilities, such as autism, but they do not have training in mental health issues, such as anxiety. Conversely, many mental health professionals don't have training and experience in working with children with developmental disabilities and mental health issues. This is unfortunate, as the two often occur concurrently in the same child. There are increasing efforts, including in our own work, to bring these two, sometimes disparate fields together.

Behavior therapists often have extensive experience in tracking behavior changes and can be very helpful in monitoring the impact of treatment. For phobia treatment it is generally quite clear to all involved when there is progress, when the child does not fall apart during a thunderstorm, loses graciously in a game or sits through a dentist appointment without distress, so spending a lot of time taking data is not usually required. However, subtle changes, such as shorter, less intense distress that has evolved gradually can be more difficult to note, and data can be very helpful in documenting those changes. Further, if no change is taking place, it is equally important to alter the treatment, by tweaking the model in this book or by using other methods alone or together.

Collaborating with psychopharmacologists

For some children, medication can be helpful in reducing baseline anxiety. At what age one tries medications, which medication to try, or even whether to use medication at all are all issues that vary a great deal from family to family, within families, from doctor to doctor and also culturally and regionally.

It is important for families who are considering medication to find a healthcare professional who can work closely with them and understand their perspectives and concerns. Sometimes medications are prescribed for other conditions that can impact anxiety, such as sleep.

Over the past couple of decades, psychotropic medications have become increasingly more specific and targeted in their usage and effects and have fewer side effects than older medications. And this is a rapidly changing and evolving specialty, so it's best to work with a psychopharmocologist who stays very current with the literature in the field. If medications are helpful for a child at a specific point in their development they may not be needed at a later point. Anxiety and specific phobias can come and go with age and development and as life circumstances change.

If a child has been prescribed medication to help with phobias it will be important to work closely with the prescriber and communicate about your tracking of the symptoms you are trying to improve.

APPENDIX

UNBUNDLING PHOBIAS
Ideas for Gradual Exposure

Sometimes the hardest part is getting started. Before plunging into a treatment regimen that will take weeks and may take months, one has to first figure out how to unbundle a child's phobia. How can you reduce washing hair to several separate components and engage in gradual exposure? Until now you probably washed your child's hair as fast as you could as she squirmed and screamed, dreading the next time. And what is causing your child's extreme fear of dogs, all dogs, large and small, barking and non-barking? You can't possibly avoid every dog, every day.

Through working with many patients over the years with similar phobias, we have developed an assortment of inventive ways to reduce feared experiences to small manageable bits or components that can then be combined with elements that are not objectionable at all and are often fun to reduce a child's fear. Of course in this model, exactly how you unbundle a phobia and the steps you take for gradual exposure will be individualized based on what you think are likely culprits stressing the child, the people and experiences your child enjoys or finds soothing, and especially how the child responds to you and others involved in treatment.

Remember: the goal is to get the child interested and engaged, but not upset or scared.

The ideas that follow are not intended as formulas or recipes, but rather as catalysts that will spark your own creativity as you tackle and unbundle your child's phobias. Below we have included fear triggers that we didn't touch upon in the case studies. To get ideas for unbundling phobias that are not in this list, you can also refer back to Chapters 4–8, which may describe phobias more like the ones you are trying to address.

Fear of washing hair in the bathtub or shower

— Do pretend hair-washing with dolls, stuffed animals, action figures, yourself, or other family members. Make the toys (or real people) pretend not to like it in a playful exaggerated way. First do it without water and far away from the tub, then in an empty tub with clothes on, then use a very small amount of water. Use pretend then real washing items (e.g. cup; visor; shampoo container).

— Use ridiculously tiny amounts of water as you pretend, to add humor and decrease fear, such as putting a small amount in a turkey baster, teaspoon or child's medicine dropper (make sure child understands it is not medicine).

— Pretend first far away from the tub, then closer to and then in the bathtub to wash just one hair (yours, the doll's, the figure, etc.) without shampoo, then with a tiny bit of shampoo. Then one more hair and so on. Make this funny!

— Pretend to wash your hair, your child's, or the doll's, in the pool or lake or even the ocean, if the child enjoys swimming and you have access to the water. Add in real props. Let the child pretend to wash your hair or the doll hair in a pool or lake.

— Make videos of someone close to your child (parent; sibling; favorite babysitter) washing their own hair (wear clothes or a bathing suit), playfully "hamming it up," pretending not to like it and then liking it. Use the child's favorite music as the soundtrack of your videos.[1]*

— Find videos on YouTube or other video sites of children having their hair washed and enjoying it. Always screen videos first!

Fear of sad/mad in stories, movies, and real life

This fear may occur when even small amounts of negative emotions are expressed by other people.

— In pretend do very short sad/happy alternations. Make the pretend sad symbolic enough to represent sad, but without much emotional expression (e.g. put hands quickly to eyes in a tear rubbing gesture). If the child thinks it's amusing as you alternate facial expressions see if you can get the child to initiate your face changing (e.g. by saying "Happy!" "Sad").

— Use animals, characters from TV or movies (Elmo, Mickey Mouse) LEGO figures, Mr. Potatohead, original Play-Doh people if you are artistic or whatever the child knows and likes and make the figures act out/display different emotions. As you do this, you can add in quick, quiet verbal cues ("Uh oh. He's so sad. Now he's HAPPY!") and accentuate your own corresponding facial expressions. Express a little fear or distress, especially at first, giving the child control so he can dial it up and you can express more emotion, or down if he gets upset. You can also draw various expressions on toys using erasable marker. Tinker with ways to express and

---

1   For any of these steps, if the child thinks it is funny and you have a way to do it, make a video the child can watch over and over.

acknowledge emotions, finding ways to increase the child's involvement and enjoyment while also increasing exposures.

— Draw a happy face on one side of a circle and a sad face on the other. If the child can't tolerate a drawing of a sad face, draw a neutral face or just leave one side blank. Flip the paper from one side to the other quickly saying "Happy!" "NOT happy" "Happy!" "Not happy." If the child thinks it's amusing as you alternate facial expressions see if you can get the child to initiate by saying "Happy!" "Sad" and comply with her requests.

— Intensify and expand the emotional expressions in the drawings and/or in your pretending. Add crying sounds when you pretend you (or a doll) is sad; add tears to the sad face.

— See if the child is interested in looking at still photographs of happy and sad babies and children or faces expressing other emotions (google images has large numbers of faces).

— Experiment with watching videos of laughing and crying babies and children. If the child is distressed when babies cry, try turning the sound off. Try playing the child's favorite music at the same time. If you find one clip the child likes, watch it together many times. Pause the video and allow the child to call the shots, i.e. whether to let it play, how loud to turn up the volume, etc.

Fear of seeing foods, trying new foods, and touching various textures

While many children are picky eaters, some have intense negative responses to seeing, touching, and smelling a range of common foods, even gagging or vomiting. This may be due to a child's past medical condition that may have negatively impacted their feeding experiences or delayed oral feeding, for example, a child who had been fed via feeding tube for a prolonged period. Sometimes children who have a hard time chewing and swallowing food due to oral motor difficulties develop fears as a result of the sensation of choking or actually choking on certain textures.

It is important to make sure the child has had a medical work-up and is cleared to eat whatever foods you present before beginning to work on the emotional aspects of eating, such as reducing anxiety and increasing comfort with a greater range of foods and textures. It is also important to decide if food is, in fact, a major problem. Eating a narrow range of foods and being extremely picky about colors, textures, and other food characteristics are not uncommon, especially during early childhood. If the child's pediatrician is not concerned and if the avoidance of some foods are not creating problems at school or at home, it might not need to be treated. But if the child is gagging at school when others are eating typical snack foods or can't sit at the table with the family or avoids even touching common toys and materials with certain textures, such as Play-Doh, rubber toys or glue), then it may be worth treating.

There are many hospital-based feeding teams, often comprised of occupational and/or speech therapists who are feeding specialists and can be very helpful in solving feeding problems.

Here are some additional unbundling and gradual exposure strategies:

— Use fake/play food representing foods that the child likes as well as foods that the child fears or those that elicit a gagging response. Pretend to eat and like ("Mmmm... Yummy!") or not like ("Eww...Yucky!") them and include them in imaginary play routines. For foods the child doesn't like, try pretending to "throw them away" in the trash with exaggerated disgust.

— Include familiar and favorite dolls and stuffed animals in these routines.

— Add in silly non-food items if the child thinks it is funny (the dinosaur eats your shoe and says "YUCK!" Batman makes soup out of checkers or LEGO).

— If the child finds this kind of play funny, add in some real food items very gradually and in very small amounts. For example, put a small amount of real yogurt on top of plastic toy yogurt and pretend to throw it away with exaggerated disgust).

— Once there is real food involved pretend to put a small amount on your lips and be very hesitant and add exaggerated disgust if the child thinks this is funny.

— At this point, see if the child will be open to putting some on his own hands/face/tongue.

Fear of new or different kinds of clothing

Some children become intensely distressed about new clothes that are nonetheless necessary. Children outgrow shoes with lightning speed. New pants and shirts feel, fit and fasten differently from their old ones. Children who live in seasonal climates may have season changes, which means they have to wear seasonally appropriate clothing such as hats (itchy), mittens (confining), boots (hard to put on) in the winter, and shorts and short sleeve shirts (too much skin exposed) in the summer. Here are some ways to use unbundling and gradual exposure for these fears:

— Keep the new clothing around—in the toy box, under the bed, in the sofa cushions—wherever the child will see it and either get used to it relatively fast or remove it and in the process, get used to it (see Chapter 9).

— For children who find it interesting and/or funny, pretend to put on the clothing item on yourself and take it off with playful exaggerated distress. If this gets a laugh, do it as many times as the child is interested or when they request it.

— See if the child thinks it is funny if you put the item in the wrong place. (Put new shoes on your head and let them fall off or "sneeze" them off; put mittens on your feet, etc.) Be as silly as you can create fun games that involve the dreaded new clothes, thereby removing their "toxicity."

— Once the child gets more used to playing with the items, experiment with starting to put them on the child, but remove them before the child does. If the child tries to get them off right away, be very obliging ("That's right. NO mittens!" speaking for the child if the child isn't talking) taking them off and throwing them to the floor, then start to put them on the child again, as long as she seems interested and open to it. Sometimes this works best when you make clear indications that you are not actually going to force the child to put it on the item on, such as putting it in the wrong place on the child. (Put socks on ears; shoes on their hands), and do it in an unpressured situation, when the child doesn't actually have to be dressed.

— Getting comfortable in short sleeves and shorts after being bundled up in the winter can be difficult for some children. First try rolling up sleeves and pant legs so the child gets used to having exposed skin while still wearing their familiar, comfortable clothing. If the child objects, put them down immediately, then roll them up a little, then roll them back down, making a game out of it. You can do this with your own clothing too.

— Some children are more comfortable wearing the same shirt every day and it can be very traumatic when it has to be washed. Think about Linus and his blanket! Some children will only wear shirts with a certain picture or logo. One solution is buying multiples of the same shirt or pair of pants. If this works, there is no need to think of it as a problem; usually children outgrow this. But if the child's distress is intense when you have to switch to different clothes, and if the child's range is too narrow to be practical, it is a problem and targeting it using the strategies outlined can be effective.

Fears of wearing new glasses, hearing aids, or braces

Many children adapt to wearing therapeutic items surprisingly quickly, whereas other children find them unpleasant at best—and sometimes, absolutely unbearable. The clinic providing the device may make suggestions and outline strategies to help your child adapt. If the child is objecting it's important to first make sure the device fits properly, is the correct prescription and is the best match available regarding material/design for your child. Fortunately, increasingly comfortable materials and smaller and less obtrusive devices are constantly being developed. There are some additional strategies which make the gradual exposure and adaptation process less uncomfortable and possibly pleasant. Sometimes heightened sensory sensitivity adds to the negative emotional experience, as well as the changed, even if improved, physical experience or enhanced ability resulting from the equipment. Sometimes just having these new "things" on causes fear. Often it's a combination.

— Introduce toy versions of the appliance and put them on dolls or action figures the child likes, and/or put them on you. If you can't find actual toy versions, make some with paper cardboard, fabric or Play-Doh.

— In playing with these toy representations, put them on yourself and pull them off as the child does, in a way that interests and amuses the child. Repeat this if the child hands them back to you.

— Add in some real devices (eye glasses; hearing aids) but be sure not to damage them. Pretend you're uncomfortable when you take them off and put them on.

— Include the device in your play routine so the child gets used to simply having it around, as long as this is safe. This is especially important with children who are not yet able to distinguish real objects from representational ones.

— Purchase or create large or silly versions of the device, such as costume glasses, big rubber or cardboard cut-out ears, or clay hearing aids. You can add these to your play routine, putting them on/taking them off and taking some photos or a movie of you and/or the child sporting silly versions of the real devices.

— If you think extrasensory sensitivity is part of the fear or phobia, help the child become accustomed to smaller, lighter or less obtrusive objects that are similar or can be used on or near the same body part. For example, play with cotton balls and place them next to the child's hearing aid, or play with light sunglass frames without lenses.

Getting water, dirt or food on clothing or body

While many children enjoy activities such as running through the sprinkler, others find it uncomfortable and are afraid of getting splashed accidentally. Some children get extremely upset if they get even a tiny bit of water or food on their clothing, from rain, a puddle or a spilled drink. This can be especially problematic in the car if you are driving and the child is in the back seat screaming as their juice spilled a little onto their pants. One child who arrived at our office for an appointment was terribly distressed and wanted to go home because it rained unexpectedly and he got a little wet. Hands covered in paint, glue or food can also cause distress.

— Play around with getting tiny amounts (invisible to begin with) of water on your own shoes, pants, shirt. Make a shape, a circle or a smiley face, with your finger by "finger painting" with water on your shoes. It seems like magic to watch it disappear together, then make it again.

— If the child is interested in this, try it first on their shoes or jacket, something they don't feel the wet from and can easily see. Then try it on their clothing or encourage them to.

— Do water finger painting on each other's hands, legs, arms.

— If the child is fine with this kind of play, start doing tiny pretend "splashing" with the tiniest amount of water, onto a figure, a doll, yourself, look surprised and wipe it off.

— Pretend to spill a full cup of water from a toy cup the child has just filled with toy juice/milk/water. Pretend to spill it on your clothes, pretend to be upset, wipe it off and be happy. If the child finds this funny do it a lot, see if the child will pretend to spill on you. See if the child will let you pretend to spill on him.

— Add a very small amount of water into the above toy cup and continue the play scenario.

— Enlist a sibling or peer who doesn't have these fears to ham it up with you and splash each other, but not so wild or wet that the child with the fear becomes distressed.

REFERENCES

American Psychiatric Association (2013) *Diagnostic and Statistical Manual of Mental Disorders* (5th ed). Washington, DC: American Psychiatric Association.

Beck, A.T. (1970) "Cognitive therapy: Nature and relation to behavior therapy." *Behavior Therapy 1*, 184–200.

Beck, A.T. (1976) *Cognitive Therapy and the Emotional Disorders*. New York:, NY Meridian.

Forbidden Games (French: *Jeux interdits*) (1952) Film, directed by René Clément. Based on the novel by François Boyer.

Cochrane Collaboration (2009) *Exercise in Prevention and Treatment of Anxiety and Depression among Children and Young People* (Review) 1. The Cochrane Collaboration, New York, NY: John Wiley.

Cohen, S. (2004) "Social relationships and health." *American Psychologist 11*, 676–682.

Cryan, J.F. and Holmes, A. (2005) "Model organisms: The ascent of mouse: Advances in modeling human depression and anxiety." *Nature Reviews Drug Discovery 4*, 775–790.

Davis D.M. and Hayes J.A. (2011) "What are the benefits of mindfulness? A practice review of psychotherapy-related research." *Psychotherapy 48*, 198–208.

Dugan, E.M., Snow, M.S. and Crowe, S.R. (2010) "Working with young children affected by hurricane Katrina: Two case studies in play therapy." *Child and Adolescent Mental Health 15*, 1, 52–55.

Ellis, A. (1957) "Rational psychotherapy and individual psychology." *Journal of Individual Psychology 13*, 38–44.

Ferber, R. (2006) *Solve your Child's Sleep Problems*. New, revised, and expanded edition. New York, NY: Simon & Schuster.

Fogel, A. (1993) *Developing Through Relationships*. Chicago, IL: University of Chicago Press.

Gaberson, K. (1995) "The effect of humorous and musical distraction on preoperative anxiety." *AORN Journal 62*, 784–791.

Garber, K., Visootsak, J. and Warren, S. (2008) "Fragile-X syndrome." *European Journal of Human Genetics 16*, 666–672.

Gil, E. and Terr, L.C. (2013) *Working with Children to Heal Interpersonal Trauma: The Power of Play.* New York, NY: Guilford Press.

Haggin, P. (2012) "Why is scary music scary? Here's the science." *Time Magazine,* June 2012.

Hayes, S.C., Follette, V.M. and Linehan, M.M. (2011) *Mindfulness and Acceptance: Expanding the Cognitive-Behavioral Tradition.* New York, NY: Guilford Press.

Herring, M.P., O'Connor, P.J. and Dishman, R.K. (2010) "The effect of exercise training on anxiety symptoms among patients: a systematic review." *Archives of Internal Medicine 170,* 321–331.

Hilton, C.L., Cumpata, K., Klorh, C., Gaetke, S., Artner, A., Johnson, H. and Dobbs, S. (2014) "Effects of exergaming on executive function and motor skills in children with autism spectrum disorder: a pilot study." *American Journal of Occupational Therapy 68,* 1, 57–65.

Hobson, J.A., Hobson, P.R, Malik S., Bargiota, K. and Caló, S. (2013) "The relation between social engagement and pretend play in autism." *British Journal of Developmental Psychology 31,* 1, 114–127.

Hobson, J.A., Hobson, R.P., Cheung, Y. and Calo, S. (2014) "Symbolizing as interpersonally grounded shifts in meaning: Social play in children with and without autism." *Journal of Autism and Developmental Disorders 45,* 1, 42–52.

Jennett, H.K. and Hagopian, L.P. (2008) "Identifying empirically supported treatments for phobic avoidance in individuals with intellectual disabilities." *Behavior Therapy 39,* 151–161.

Jones, M.C. (1924) "A laboratory study of fear: The case of Peter." *Pedagogical Seminary 31,* 308–315.

Katz, T. and Malow, A.B. (2014) *Solving Sleep Problems in Children with Autism Spectrum Disorders: A Guide for Frazzled Families.* Bethesda, MD: Woodbine.

Kendall, P.C. and Hedtke, K. (2006) *Coping Cat Workbook,* 2nd edn. Ardmore: Workbook Publishing.

Kessler, R.C., Berglund, P., Demler, O., Jin, R., Merikangas, K.R. and Walters, E.E. (2005) "Lifetime prevalence and age-of-onset distributions of DSM-IV disorders in the national comorbidity survey replication." *Archives of General Psychiatry 62,* 593.

Lang, R., Register, A., Lauderdale, S., Ashbuagh, K. and Haring, A. (2010) "Treatment of anxiety in autism spectrum disorders using cognitive behaviour therapy: A systematic review." *Developmental Neurorehabilitation 13,* 1, 53–63.

Levine, K., Chedd, N. and Bauch, D. (2009) "Social-affective diet: launching a concept." *Autism Spectrum Quarterly* Fall, 24–29.

Leyfer, O.T., Folstein, S., Bacalman, S., Davis, N.O., Dinh, E., Morgan, J., *et al.* (2006) "Comorbid psychiatric disorders in children with autism: Interview development and rates of disorders." *Journal of Autism and Developmental Disorders 36,* 849–861.

Lovorn, M.G. (2008) "Humour in the classroom: The benefits of laughing while we learn." *Journal of Education and Human Development 2,* 1, 1–12.

Maskey, M., Lowry, J., Rodgers, J., McConachie, H. and Parr, J.R. (2014) "Reducing specific phobia/fear in young people with autism spectrum disorders (ASDs) through a virtual reality environment intervention." *PLoS ONE 9,* 7, e100374.

Moog, C. and McHenry, I. (2014) *The Autism Playbook for Teens: Imagination-Based Mindfulness Activities to Calm Yourself, Build Independence, and Connect with Others.* The Instant Help Solutions Series. Oakland, CA: New Harbinger Publications.

Salzman, A. and Santorelli, S. (2014). *A Still Quiet Place: A Mindfulness Program for Teaching Children and Adolescents to Ease Stress and Difficult Emotions.* Oakland, CA: New Harbinger Publications.

Schacht, S. and Stewart, B.J. (1990) "What's funny about statistics? A technique for reducing student anxiety." *Teaching Sociology 18,* 1, 52–56.

Sukhodolsky, D.G., Bloch, M.H., Panza, K.E. and Reichow, B. (2013) "Cognitive-behavioral therapy for anxiety in children with high-functioning autism: A meta-analysis." *Pediatrics 132,* 5.

Sullivan, P.F., Magnusson, C., Reichenberg, A., Boman, M., Dalman, C. and Davidson, M. (2012) "Family history of schizophrenia and bipolar disorder as risk factors for autism." *General Psychiatry 69,* 11, 1099–1103.

Thoits, P. (2011) "Mechanisms linking social ties and support to physical and mental health." *Journal of Health and Social Behavior 52,* 145–161.

Tronick E. and Beeghly, M. (2011) "Infants' meaning-making and the development of mental health problems." *American Psychologist 66,* 2, 107–119.

Umberson, D. and Montez, J.K. (2010) "Social relationships and health: A flashpoint for health policy." *Journal of Health and Social Behavior 5,* (Suppl): S54–66.

Van Steensel, F.J., Bogels, S.M. and Perrin, S. (2011) "Anxiety disorders in children and adolescents with autistic disorders: a meta-analysis." *Clinical Child and Family Psychology Review 14,* 3, 302–317.

Wagner, A.P. (2013) *Up and Down the Worry Hill: A Children's Book about Obsessive-Compulsive Disorder and its Treatment.* Apex, NC: Lighthouse Press.

Wolpe, J. (1954) "Reciprocal inhibition as the main basis of psychotherapeutic effects." *Archives of Neurology and Psychiatry 72,* 2, 205–226.

Wolpe, J. (1958) *Psychotherapy by Reciprocal Inhibition.* Stanford, CA: Stanford University Press.

Woodruff-Borden, J., Kistler, D., Henderson, D.R., Crawford, N.A., and Mervis, C.B. (2010) "Longitudinal course of anxiety in children and adolescents with Williams' syndrome." *American Journal of Medical Genetics Part C Seminar in Medical Genetics 154C,* 2, 277–290.

INDEX

Page references in *italic* indicate figures.